Real Food
from your
Food
Processor

Daphne Metland

foulsham
LONDON • NEW YORK • TORONTO • SYDNEY

foulsham

The Publishing House, Bennetts Close,
Cippenham, Berks, SL1 5AP

ISBN 0-572-02608-0

Printed in Great Britain by Cox & Wyman Ltd, Reading.

CONTENTS

INTRODUCTION

Food processors are powerful, hard-working machines that can chop, purée, slice, shred and mix most foods in seconds. They take most of the hard work out of cooking, leaving the enjoyable parts for you to do and expanding your culinary repertoire into the bargain.

This book aims to release the potential of your food processor. There is no point it sitting in the cupboard or on the work surface taking up space and not earning its keep. With this book, you can ensure that you are really getting the best out of its capabilities. If you are new to food processor cooking, you'll learn all about it. If you use yours only to blend soups, you'll find out how many other options it offers you. Even if you are experienced, you'll discover that you can produce dishes that would normally be considered quite difficult, but with a processor are quick and easy. That means you can have more time to yourself and cook more interesting dishes.

Most machines are very similar and techniques vary little from machine to machine, although when first using your food processor it is worth reading thoroughly the instruction booklet that comes with your particular machine. That way, you will not miss out on any special features of your machine. The power of various machines does vary slightly, which influences how quickly the food is processed, but since the most common problem is overprocessing, I have quoted the minimum processing times in the recipes. It is then easy to pulse for an extra few seconds if necessary. Once you have puréed a mixture you meant to chop, there's not much you can do about it! Experience will soon guide you in judging the correct time for your particular machine.

So don't hide your processor in a cupboard – it is likely to stay there. Leave it out on the work surface and you'll quickly learn to make use of it to undertake the whole range of jobs that it excels at. My food processor has pride of place in my kitchen; I hope yours will too.

YOUR FOOD PROCESSOR

This chapter will outline the components of your food processor and how to use them.

FOOD PROCESSOR ATTACHMENTS

All food processors have a metal blade, and at least one slicing and one grating disc. These three attachments are mentioned in the recipes in this book. Most also have plastic blades and other discs. This outline gives you basic information on which blade or disc is suitable for which job, but do check the instruction booklet supplied with your machine to make sure you do not have an extra attachment specifically designed for a particular task. Try them out before you start on an actual recipe so you know how they work.

Metal Blade

This is the most versatile of the fitments. It is used for chopping cooked and uncooked meats, fish and poultry, and for reducing these to a purée or paste. Vegetables such as onions, carrots and potatoes and fruits can be chopped or puréed. It also makes breadcrumbs and sauces, and can be used for chopping and grinding nuts, and for combining cake, bread and biscuit mixtures.

Some processors have a plastic blade which is used instead of the metal blade for cake, bread and biscuit mixtures.

Slicing Disc

Hard vegetables and fruits such as cabbage, raw potatoes, carrots, leeks, apples and pears can all be sliced with the slicing disc. Foods should be trimmed to fit the feed tube and held in place with the pusher, not your fingers! Tall items, such as carrots and leeks, need to be stacked in the feed tube so that they do not fall over while being processed as this will change the finished shape of the food. Some foods will need processing in batches as the bowl will quickly fill with sliced food.

Tinned meats can be sliced if they are chilled in the fridge for an hour or so before use. Take care not to push down too hard with the pusher. It is also possible to slice raw meats thinly, but only if still partly frozen. Even softer foods such as firm strawberries, peaches, tomatoes and cooked potatoes can be sliced with care.

Remember that the way you stack the food in the feed tube determines the shape of the finished slices. Apple halves positioned horizontally will make crescent-shaped slices, while those placed vertically will make semi-circular slices. Long foods, such as bananas, carrots and courgettes (zucchini), can be sliced into circles or long strips, as you prefer. Use the pusher as a guide for measuring the correct size of food to go through the feed tube.

Sometimes pieces of food catch on the slicing or grating discs and this is quite normal. If a great deal of food catches on the discs, however, the food was probably not loaded correctly in the feed tube.

Some machines have thick and thin slicing discs.

Grating Disc

The grating disc will cope with most hard vegetables as well as cheeses and chocolate. It is ideal for salad foods, and ingredients such as carrots, beetroot (red beet), celeriac (celery root) and cucumber can all be grated successfully. Many families find it convenient to grate enough cheese for several days and store it in a plastic box in the fridge so that it always ready for packed lunches and snacks.

Some machines have fine and coarse grating discs.

Whisks

Some processors have whisk attachments, but it is important to remember that the amount of air that can be introduced into foods such as egg whites and cream is limited by the fact that a processor has a lid. The whisking is usually sufficient for mousses but not always suitable for meringues or for making cream stiff enough to pipe; it does depend on the machine. Check the instruction leaflet for the suitability of the whisk attachment for various uses.

Recipes in this book suggest that egg whites can be whisked by hand or in the processor, but it is also possible to fold in egg whites by adding them to the processor and operating the machine for a few seconds only.

Other Attachments

Many companies offer other discs and attachments for food processors. Their uses are more specific than those listed above, and can therefore replace them if appropriate. Many machines have a chipping disc, which may well be popular with families. It works in exactly the same way as the slicing and grating discs.

Some machines have other attachments such as juice extractors or even pasta makers that fit to the motor base.

Cleaning Your Food Processor

Bowls and lids can be washed in the sink, and many are dishwasher-proof, but do check in the instruction booklet. Blades and discs need to be cleaned with a small brush, preferably under running water. A small bottle brush will help to clean the inside of the plastic centre, where it fits on to the motor base. Dry all parts well and leave the lid off when re-assembling to allow air to circulate.

The motor base should never be immersed in water. Unplug and wipe clean with a barely damp cloth.

STORING YOUR FOOD PROCESSOR

If you keep your food processor in a cupboard you'll never use it. Keep it on the work surface, but store the blades and discs safely – perhaps in a box in a cupboard, especially if there are children in the house. Some companies make storage racks for the various attachments, others cleverly store the attachments inside the bowl. Never store the attachments in your cutlery drawer.

FOOD PROCESSOR BASICS

A food processor can take much of the hard work out of preparing foods but there are a few simple rules you need to follow in order to ensure that it makes your life as easy as possible.

THE RIGHT LOAD

Avoid overloading the machine. The bowl capacity limits the amount of food that can be processed at any one time and too much food will cause uneven processing. This is noticeable as large lumps of food sitting on top of the processed food. Process large quantities of food in batches and transfer the finished food to a bowl while the next load is being processed.

Machine capacities vary, but most will cope with between 225–350 g/8–12 oz of meat, a three-egg cake mixture or up to 450 g/1 lb of bread dough.

Soft mixtures, such as cake mixtures and pâtés, will need to be scraped down during processing to ensure a completely smooth mixture. This can usually be done when other ingredients are being added to avoid having to lift off the processor lid too often.

Food processors can cope with most foods, but whole grains, coffee beans and ice cubes are generally not recommended. Check your instruction booklet.

THE RIGHT TIMING

Because food processors are powerful, it is easy to overprocess foods, ending up with a puréed mixture instead of a chopped one, for example. Onions can be chopped in three seconds or puréed in five, and meat can be minced (ground coarsely) in eight seconds and ground to a paste in 12. It is very important, therefore, to keep an eye on the food in the processor and stop to check the condition of the food during the processing time. Never leave the machine unattended and always err on the side of too little rather than too much time. It is easy to give the mixture an extra second or two. Most machines have a pulse button, which you can use for short processing times rather than switching on and off, but even if your machine does not have a pulse button, it is easy to turn the machine on and off quickly.

Machines do vary slightly in the time they take to process foods, depending on how powerful they are, the size of the bowl and the quantity of food. All the recipes in this book give approximate timings achieved simply by counting slowly when processing, followed by a description of what the food should look like when it is ready, for example: 'Process for 10 seconds until finely chopped'. Just follow that advice and you can't go far wrong.

THE RIGHT ORDER

For most recipes, you can minimise washing-up by preparing foods in the right order. Make up the foods that will cause the least mess first. For instance, prepare the pastry (paste) first if you are making a quiche, then prepare the filling so that you don't need to wash the bowl after you have made the pastry. You can just scrape the bowl with a spatula before you add the filling ingredients.

All the recipes in this book have been written with this in mind, so it is usually only necessary to wash the bowl and attachments at the end of the recipe. There are a few exceptions, of course, particularly with foods such as beetroot (red beet), which will stain everything it comes into contact with. Often, the remaining fragments of food actually enhance the next step of the recipe, for instance when making a salad dressing after slicing the vegetables to go into the salad.

CONTROLS

Using a food processor could not be simpler. Most have a speed control and an on–off switch. You simply select a fast or slow speed and switch on. Since foods are processed very quickly, switch on for the shortest period of time, check the food, then process again as necessary.

Most machines also have a pulse button, which is ideal for shorter processing times.

On the whole, food processors are relatively quiet in operation, but some foods, particularly hard ones like nuts and chocolate, will make a great deal of noise while being processed. To ensure minimum noise, always place the machine on a firm worktop and avoid overloading it, which will cause excessive vibration; some machines also tend to 'walk' if overloaded.

FOOD PROCESSOR SAFETY

Processor blades are sharp; they have to be to do their job. Just follow a few simple safety rules when using your machine. They may seem obvious, but it does not hurt to remind yourself to be careful.

◇ Do not touch the blades or discs while they are still revolving. Food processors switch off if the lid is removed, but it can take a few seconds for the blades to stop turning once the machine is turned off.

◇ Never reach in and pick up the blade or disc by the sharp cutting edge. Instead, lift the bowl off the motor base, so loosening the attachment, then pick up blades carefully by the plastic centre piece or discs by the rim.

◇ Never leave blades or discs in the washing-up bowl. Stand them safely on the work surface where they can be easily seen until you are ready to wash them up.

◇ Never put blades in the cutlery tray of a dishwasher.

◇ Store the blades safely, never in a drawer or loose in a cupboard.

NOTES ON THE RECIPES

◇ The following symbols are used at the beginning of recipes:

Use the metal blade.   Use the grating disc.

Use the slicing disc.   Suitable for freezing.

◇ Do not mix metric, imperial and American measures. Use one set only. American terms are given in brackets.

◇ Spoon measurements are level: 1 tsp = 5 ml; 1 tbsp = 15 ml.

◇ Eggs are medium unless otherwise stated. Can and packet sizes are approximate.

◇ Always wash, peel, core and seed, if necessary, fresh fruit and vegetables before use. Ensure that all produce is as fresh as possible and in good condition.

◇ If you are using the feed tube, trim vegetables to shape.

◇ Always use fresh herbs unless dried are specifically called for. If you use dried herbs, use half the quantity stated.

◇ The recipes give approximate processing times, calculated by counting slowly, and a description of what the food should look like when processed. Machines vary slightly in the time they take to process foods, so check the condition of the food during the processing time and adjust if necessary to suit your own machine.

◇ Always preheat the oven (unless it is fan-assisted) and cook on the centre shelf. Adjust cooking times and temperatures to suit your own appliance.

SOUPS

The processor is perfect for making soups as it can be used to prepare vegetables and other ingredients, and also to create finely puréed, or coarsely chopped, thick winter soups. Crusty bread makes a tasty accompaniment, or you can sprinkle the soup with grated cheese or crisp croûtons.

For an extra-quick vegetable soup, finely chop a selection of vegetables in the processor, mix with stock and cook for 10 minutes, then purée and season before serving.

Any leftover foods can be quickly sliced, grated or finely chopped and added to home-made soups for extra flavouring.

TOMATO AND ORANGE SOUP

—— SERVES 4 ——

🐟 ❄ 4 MONTHS	METRIC	IMPERIAL	AMERICAN
Tomatoes	450 g	1 lb	1 lb
Potato, cut into chunks	1	1	1
Carrot, cut into chunks	1	1	1
Chicken or vegetable stock	900 ml	1½ pts	3¾ cups
A few sprigs of basil			
Salt and freshly ground black pepper			
Juice of ½ orange			
Single (light) cream	150 ml	¼ pt	⅔ cup

① Place the tomatoes, potato and carrot chunks, stock and basil in a pan, bring to the boil, then simmer for about 20 minutes until the vegetables are tender. Strain, reserving the cooking liquid.

② Fit the metal blade. Process the vegetables for about 15 seconds until smooth, then return to the pan, stir in the orange juice and season to taste with salt and pepper. Stir in the cream and heat through gently.

PREPARATION AND COOKING TIME: 30 MINUTES

BACON AND SWEETCORN CHOWDER

—— SERVES 4–6 ——

	METRIC	IMPERIAL	AMERICAN
Large onion, quartered	I	I	I
Oil	15 ml	I tbsp	I tbsp
Bacon, rinded	175 g	6 oz	6 oz
Celery stick, cut into chunks	I	I	I
Small green (bell) pepper, cut into chunks	I	I	I
Potato, quartered	I	I	I
Dry sherry	15 ml	I tbsp	I tbsp
Chicken stock	600 ml	I pt	2½ cups
Canned or frozen sweetcorn (corn)	225 g	8 oz	8 oz
Milk	300 ml	½ pt	I¼ cups
Salt and freshly ground black pepper			

① Fit the metal blade. Process the onion for a few seconds in short bursts until evenly chopped.

② Heat the oil in a large pan and fry (sauté) the onion for 5 minutes until softened but not browned.

③ Meanwhile, process the bacon for 4–5 seconds until evenly chopped, then add it to the pan. Process the celery and pepper for 4–5 seconds until evenly chopped, then add it to the pan. Process the potato for a few seconds until evenly chopped, then add it to the pan.

④ Pour in the sherry and stir well, then pour in the stock, bring to the boil and simmer for 10–15 minutes until the vegetables are tender.

⑤ Add the sweetcorn and simmer for 10 minutes.

⑥ Add the milk and season generously with salt and pepper. Heat gently for a further 5 minutes without allowing the soup to boil.

PREPARATION AND COOKING TIME: 30 MINUTES

FRENCH ONION SOUP

—— SERVES 4 ——

⊕ ⟲ ❄ 2 MONTHS	METRIC	IMPERIAL	AMERICAN
Onions	450 g	1 lb	1 lb
Butter or margarine	100 g	4 oz	½ cup
Oil	15 ml	1 tbsp	1 tbsp
Beef stock	1.2 litres	2 pts	5 cups
Potatoes	2	2	2
Strong hard cheese, roughly crumbled	50 g	2 oz	½ cup
French mustard	5 ml	1 tsp	1 tsp
Chopped parsley	15 ml	1 tbsp	1 tbsp
Salt and freshly ground black pepper			
Baguette, thickly sliced	½	½	½

① Fit the slicing disc and slice the onions.

② Heat half the butter or margarine with the oil and fry (sauté) the onions gently until soft and golden brown. Add the stock and bring to the boil.

③ Meanwhile, trim the potatoes to fit the feed tube and slice. Add to the stock, return to the boil, then simmer for 15 minutes.

④ Fit the metal blade. Drop the cheese on to the blade, then add the mustard, parsley and remaining butter or margarine and process until mixed. Season with salt and pepper.

⑤ Spread the cheese mixture over the baguette slices and toast under the grill (broiler).

⑥ Serve the soup in warmed bowls and float the golden-brown cheese toasts on top.

Freezing tip: Freeze without the bread slices.

PREPARATION AND COOKING TIME: 30 MINUTES

WINTER VEGETABLE SOUP
—— SERVES 4 ——

❄ 3 MONTHS	METRIC	IMPERIAL	AMERICAN
Onion, quartered	I	I	I
Garlic clove, halved	I	I	I
Potato, quartered	I	I	I
Carrot, cut into chunks	I	I	I
Leek, cut into chunks	I	I	I
Celery stick, cut into chunks	I	I	I
Oil	15 ml	I tbsp	I tbsp
Dry sherry	45 ml	3 tbsp	3 tbsp
Chicken stock	750 ml	1¼ pts	3 cups
Chopped parsley or mixed herbs	15 ml	I tbsp	I tbsp
Salt and freshly ground black pepper			
Grated cheese or croûtons, to serve			

① Fit the metal blade. Process the onion and garlic for a few seconds until chopped. Remove from the processor.

② Process the potato, carrot, leek and celery for 6–8 seconds until coarsely chopped.

③ Heat the oil in a large pan and fry (sauté) the onion gently until softened but not browned. Add the remaining vegetables and fry for a few minutes, stirring until well mixed.

④ Add the sherry, stir and simmer for 2 minutes.

⑤ Add the stock and herbs, bring to the boil and simmer gently for 20 minutes, stirring occasionally.

⑥ Season to taste with salt and pepper and serve in warmed bowls with grated cheese or croûtons.

PREPARATION AND COOKING TIME: 30 MINUTES

VELVETY CARROT SOUP

—— SERVES 4 ——

🐟 ⊕ ❄ 3 MONTHS	METRIC	IMPERIAL	AMERICAN
Onion, quartered	1	1	1
Garlic clove, halved	1	1	1
Carrots	450 g	1 lb	1 lb
Oil	15 ml	1 tbsp	1 tbsp
Chicken stock	600 ml	1 pt	2½ cups
Sugar	2.5 ml	½ tsp	½ tsp
Salt and freshly ground black pepper			
Single (light) cream	150 ml	¼ pt	⅔ cup

① Fit the metal blade. Process the onion and garlic for a few seconds until finely chopped.

② Fit the slicing disc and slice the carrots.

③ Heat the oil in a large saucepan and gently fry (sauté) the onions and garlic until soft.

④ Stir in the carrots, then pour in the stock and sugar and season to taste with salt and pepper. Bring to the boil, then simmer for 15 minutes until the carrots are soft.

⑤ Fit the metal blade. Purée the soup in two batches.

⑥ Return the soup to the pan and reheat gently. Stir in the cream and warm through but do not allow the soup to boil.

PREPARATION AND COOKING TIME: 25 MINUTES

VICHYSSOISE

—— SERVES 4 ——

⊕ ◔ ❋ 2 MONTHS	METRIC	IMPERIAL	AMERICAN
Leeks	450 g	I lb	I lb
Celery stick	I	I	I
Butter or margarine	50 g	2 oz	¼ cup
Potatoes	3	3	3
Chicken or vegetable stock	600 ml	I pt	2½ cups
Salt and freshly ground black pepper			
Single (light) cream or milk	150 ml	¼ pt	⅔ cup
Crème fraîche, to serve			
Snipped chives, to garnish			

① Fit the slicing disc and slice the leeks and celery.

② Heat the butter or margarine in a large saucepan and gently fry (sauté) the leeks and celery for 5 minutes until softened but not browned.

③ Cut the potatoes to fit the feed tube and slice them. Add to the leeks, then stir in the stock and season to taste with salt and pepper. Bring to the boil, then simmer for 15–20 minutes until the vegetables are tender.

④ Fit the metal blade and purée the soup in two batches.

⑤ Return the soup to the pan and add the cream or milk. Heat through gently until well blended but do not allow the soup to boil.

⑥ Cool, then chill the soup and serve topped with a swirl of crème fraîche and garnished with the snipped chives.

Variation: You can serve this soup hot or cold.

PREPARATION AND COOKING TIME: 30 MINUTES

PÂTÉS AND DIPS

A food processor is perfect for making pâtés – it does all the chopping and mixing for you, and you can make the texture as coarse and chunky or as smooth and fine as you like. Remember, though, that it only takes seconds to turn everything into a purée, so err on the side of caution at first!

Dips are a breeze too – you can whizz up the ingredients literally in seconds – a real boon if you have unexpected guests.

You can make a quick, fresh taramasalata by processing a shallot, then adding 100 g/4 oz of smoked fish roe, two slices of soaked and squeezed bread, 60 ml/4 tbsp of lemon juice and 300 ml/½ pt/1¼ cups of olive oil. Add plenty of seasoning and serve with dips.

Home-made hummus is just as simple. Process two shallots and a garlic clove, then add a small, drained can of chick peas (garbanzos) with 150 ml/¼ pt/⅔ cup of plain yoghurt, 10 ml/2 tsp of lemon juice, 15 ml/1 tbsp of olive oil and 2.5 ml/½ tsp of ground cumin. Season to taste and serve.

Home-made pâtés freeze well. Slice thickly and interleaf with foil or greaseproof (waxed) paper, then overwrap and freeze. Thaw for 2–3 hours before serving.

BACON AND LIVER PÂTÉ
—— SERVES 4 ——

	METRIC	IMPERIAL	AMERICAN
Onion, quartered	I	I	I
Garlic clove, halved	I	I	I
Streaky bacon, rinded	225 g	8 oz	8 oz
Belly pork, rinded and cut into chunks	225 g	8 oz	8 oz
Lambs' liver, trimmed	225 g	8 oz	8 oz
Butter or margarine, chopped	25 g	I oz	2 tbsp
Single (light) cream	30 ml	2 tbsp	2 tbsp
Ground mace	2.5 ml	½ tsp	½ tsp
Salt and freshly ground black pepper			
Crackers or crusty bread, to serve			

① Fit the metal blade. Process the onion and garlic for 3–5 seconds until evenly chopped. Transfer to a mixing bowl.

② Put half the bacon aside. Chop the remainder roughly and add to the processor with the pork. Process for 10–15 seconds until evenly chopped. You can make the consistency coarse or fine, according to preference.

③ Add the liver and process for about 5 seconds until evenly incorporated, then add the butter or margarine, cream, mace, salt and pepper and process until well combined. Mix with the onions and garlic.

④ Stretch the reserved bacon with the back of a knife and use to line a 900 g/2 lb pâté dish. Fill with the pâté mixture and press down lightly. Cover with foil and place in a baking tin (pan). Fill the tin with hot water to come halfway up the sides of the dish.

⑤ Bake in a preheated oven at 190°C/375°F/gas mark 5 for 30 minutes.

⑥ Leave to cool in the tin, then place some weights or a can on top and chill overnight. Serve this soft-textured pâté well chilled and cut into slices, with crackers or crusty bread.

PREPARATION AND COOKING TIME: 40 MINUTES

CHICKEN AND MUSHROOM PÂTÉ

—— SERVES 6 ——

⊕ 🐟 ❄ 2 MONTHS	METRIC	IMPERIAL	AMERICAN
Mushrooms	100 g	4 oz	4 oz
Onion, quartered	1	1	1
Butter or margarine	75 g	3 oz	⅓ cup
Chicken livers	225 g	8 oz	8 oz
Dry sherry	15 ml	1 tbsp	1 tbsp
Double (heavy) cream	30 ml	2 tbsp	2 tbsp
Cooked chicken	100 g	4 oz	1 cup
Crackers or crusty rolls, to serve			

1. Fit the slicing disc and slice the mushrooms. Remove from the bowl.

2. Fit the metal blade. Process the onion for 3–4 seconds until finely chopped.

3. Heat half the butter or margarine and fry (sauté) the onion for 5 minutes until softened but not browned. Add the chicken livers and fry for 10 minutes until just cooked. Stir in the sherry, then add the cream and all but 15 ml/1 tbsp of the remaining butter or margarine.

4. Process the cooked chicken for a few seconds until finely chopped. Add the cooked chicken liver mixture and process for 7 seconds.

5. Generously grease a 450 g/1 lb pâté dish with the remaining butter or margarine and arrange the mushrooms on the base. Cover with half the pâté, top with the remaining mushrooms, then with the remaining pâté. Cover with foil and place in a baking tin (pan). Fill the tin with hot water to come halfway up the sides of the dish.

6. Bake in a preheated oven at 190°C/375°F/gas mark 5 for 30 minutes.

7. Leave to cool in the tin, then place some weights or a can on top and chill overnight. Serve this soft-textured pâté well chilled and cut into slices, with crackers or crusty bread.

PREPARATION AND COOKING TIME: 50 MINUTES

COUNTRY PÂTÉ

—— SERVES 4 ——

🍃 ❄ 6 MONTHS	METRIC	IMPERIAL	AMERICAN
Garlic clove, halved	1	1	1
Onion, quartered	1	1	1
Streaky bacon, rinded	100 g	4 oz	4 oz
Lambs' liver	225 g	8 oz	8 oz
Lean pork	225 g	8 oz	8 oz
Butter or margarine	25 g	1 oz	2 tbsp
Chopped parsley	30 ml	2 tbsp	2 tbsp
Double (heavy) cream	30 ml	2 tbsp	2 tbsp
Salt and freshly ground black pepper			
Crackers or crusty bread and mixed salad, to serve			

① Fit the metal blade. Process the garlic for 5–6 seconds until chopped, then add the onion and process for 5–6 seconds until chopped. Remove from the bowl.

② Cut the bacon roughly into pieces and process for 5–6 seconds until chopped. Add the liver and process for 4–5 seconds until chopped. Add the pork and process for 4 seconds until finely chopped.

③ Add the butter or margarine, parsley and cream and season generously with salt and pepper. Process until well mixed to your preferred consistency.

④ Press the mixture gently into a 900 g/2 lb loaf tin (pan), cover with foil and stand the dish in a roasting tin. Fill the tin with hot water to come halfway up the sides. Cover with foil and bake in a preheated oven at 180°C/350°F/gas mark 4 for 1½ hours.

⑤ Leave to cool in the tin, then place some weights or a can on top and chill overnight. Serve cut into slices, with crackers or crusty bread and a mixed salad.

PREPARATION AND COOKING TIME: 2 HOURS

SMOKED MACKEREL PÂTÉ
—— SERVES 4 ——

⊕ ◌ ❋ 3 MONTHS	METRIC	IMPERIAL	AMERICAN
Lemon	I	I	I
Smoked mackerel	225 g	8 oz	8 oz
Butter or margarine	50 g	2 oz	¼ cup
Ground mace	2.5 ml	½ tsp	½ tsp
Double (heavy) cream or crème fraîche	15 ml	I tbsp	I tbsp
Freshly ground black pepper			
Granary bread, to serve			

① Fit the slicing disc. Cut the lemon in half lengthways, then slice one half and remove from the bowl.

② Fit the metal blade. Skin the fish and cut roughly into chunks. Process for 7–8 seconds until well flaked.

③ With the motor running, drop pieces of the butter or margarine one at a time through the feed tube until they are well mixed with the mackerel.

④ Add the mace, cream or crème fraîche, the juice of the remaining half lemon and black pepper to taste. Process for 3–4 seconds until well blended.

⑤ Press gently into individual dishes and arrange the lemon slices on top. Chill for 1 hour before serving with slices of granary bread.

Freezing tip: Freeze in small portions or individual dishes. Thaw at room temperature for 3–4 hours before serving.

PREPARATION TIME: 15 MINUTES

AVOCADO AND TUNA MOUSSE
—— SERVES 4 ——

	METRIC	IMPERIAL	AMERICAN
Avocados, halved, stoned (pitted) and peeled	2	2	2
Can of tuna fish, drained	200 g	7 oz	I small
Plain yoghurt	60 ml	4 tbsp	4 tbsp
Tabasco sauce	5 ml	I tsp	I tsp
Lemon juice	10–15 ml	2–3 tsp	2–3 tsp
Freshly ground black pepper			
Toast or melba toast, to serve			

1. Fit the metal blade. Cut the avocados roughly into chunks and process for about 10 seconds until finely chopped, scraping down the sides of the bowl halfway through.

2. Add the tuna fish, yoghurt, Tabasco sauce, 10 ml/2 tsp of the lemon juice and some pepper and process for a further 10 seconds until well blended and smooth. Taste and add extra Tabasco, lemon juice and pepper to taste.

3. Chill well and serve with toast or melba toast.

PREPARATION TIME: 15 MINUTES

SALMON AND CRÈME FRAÎCHE DIP
—— SERVES 4 ——

	METRIC	IMPERIAL	AMERICAN
Crème fraîche	150 ml	¼ pt	⅔ cup
Can of salmon	100 g	4 oz	I small
Lemon juice	5 ml	I tsp	I tsp
Salt and freshly ground black pepper			
Paprika and a sprig of parsley, to garnish			
A selection of crudités or crackers, to serve			

①   Place all the ingredients in the processor and process for 5–10 seconds, depending on how smooth you want the dip.

②   Pour into a serving dish, dust with a little paprika and decorate with a sprig of parsley.

③   Serve with a selection of crudités or crackers.

PREPARATION TIME: 10 MINUTES

HOT GUACAMOLE

—— SERVES 4 ——

	METRIC	IMPERIAL	AMERICAN
Garlic cloves, halved	1	1	1
Jalapeño pepper, seeded	½	½	½
Spring onion (scallion)	1	1	1
Large avocado, peeled, halved and stoned (pitted)	1	1	1
Lemon juice	15 ml	1 tbsp	1 tbsp
Plum tomato, skinned, seeded and chopped	1	1	1
A few drops of Tabasco sauce			
Chopped coriander (cilantro)	15 ml	1 tbsp	1 tbsp
Salt and freshly ground black pepper			

①   Fit the metal blade. With the motor running, drop the garlic, pepper and spring onion through the feed tube and process for a few seconds until chopped. Add three-quarters of the avocado flesh and the lemon juice and process for 3–4 seconds until chopped. Turn into a bowl.

②   Chop the remaining avocado and stir into the bowl with the tomato, Tabasco sauce and coriander, and season to taste with salt and pepper.

③   Serve within 2 hours or the guacamole will start to discolour.

PREPARATION TIME: 15 MINUTES

DIP SELECTION

EACH RECIPE SERVES 4

For Avocado and Tomato Dip:

	METRIC	IMPERIAL	AMERICAN
Juice of I small lemon			
Avocados, peeled and stoned (pitted)	2	2	2
Garlic clove, halved	I	I	I
Crème fraîche	30 ml	2 tbsp	2 tbsp
Tomatoes, skinned and seeded	2	2	2
A few drops of Tabasco sauce			
Salt and freshly ground black pepper			

For Bacon and Butter Bean Dip:

	METRIC	IMPERIAL	AMERICAN
Rashers (slices) of streaky bacon, rinded and fried (sautéed)	4	4	4
Can of butter (lima) beans, drained	225 g	8 oz	I med
Mayonnaise	60 ml	4 tbsp	4 tbsp
Lemon juice	10 ml	2 tsp	2 tsp
Salt and freshly ground black pepper			

For Yoghurt and Stilton Dip:

	METRIC	IMPERIAL	AMERICAN
Stilton cheese, rinded and crumbled	100 g	4 oz	I cup
Plain yoghurt	150 ml	¼ pt	⅔ cup
Cream cheese	30 ml	2 tbsp	2 tbsp
Salt and freshly ground black pepper			

① Place all the ingredients into the processor and process for 5–10 seconds, depending on the ingredients, until smooth. Season to taste with salt and pepper.

② Turn out into small pots and serve garnished with sprigs of fresh herbs.

PREPARATION TIME: 10 MINUTES

There are many ways in which the processor can make it easy to create delicious snacks or light meals.

To make your own crisps, thinly slice potatoes and pat the slices dry on kitchen paper (paper towels). Deep-fry until crisp and golden, then drain well and sprinkle with salt before serving.

Leftover meats or poultry can be used to make tasty sandwich fillings. Simply mix the meat with a little butter and seasoning and purée well.

BACON AND KIDNEY ROLLS

—— SERVES 4 ——

❧ ❄ 3 MONTHS	METRIC	IMPERIAL	AMERICAN
Shallots	3	3	3
Slice of bread	½	½	½
Kidneys, trimmed	100 g	4 oz	4 oz
Dried mixed herbs	2.5 ml	½ tsp	½ tsp
A few drops of Tabasco sauce			
Tomato purée (paste)	5 ml	1 tsp	1 tsp
Rashers (slices) of streaky bacon, rinded	10	10	10
Greek salad, to serve			

① Fit the metal blade. Process the shallots for 3–4 seconds until chopped, then transfer to a mixing bowl.

② With the motor running, drop pieces of the bread through the feed tube and process into breadcrumbs, then add to the shallots.

③ Put the kidneys in the processor and pulse for a few seconds until just chopped.

④ Add the shallots, breadcrumbs, herbs, Tabasco sauce and tomato purée and process for a few seconds until just mixed.

⑤ Stretch the bacon rashers with the back of a knife. Place a large teaspoonful of the kidney mixture on the end of each rasher and roll up.

⑥ Grill (broil) under a hot grill (broiler) for 10 minutes, turning once, then serve with a Greek salad.

Freezing tip: Open-freeze the uncooked rolls until hard, then pack in freezer bags. When required, thaw at room temperature for 2 hours, then cook as in the recipe.

PREPARATION AND COOKING TIME: 20 MINUTES

STUFFED COURGETTES

—— SERVES 4 ——

✳ 🐁 ❋ 2 MONTHS	METRIC	IMPERIAL	AMERICAN
Courgettes (zucchini)	4	4	4
Mature Cheddar or other strongly flavoured cheese	100 g	4 oz	4 oz
Hard-boiled (hard-cooked) egg	1	1	1
Cooked ham, cut into pieces	100 g	4 oz	1 cup
Chopped parsley	15 ml	1 tbsp	1 tbsp
Salt and freshly ground black pepper			

① Halve the courgettes lengthways, then scoop out the flesh and leave to one side. Place the courgette shells in an ovenproof dish.

② Fit the grating disc. Grate the cheese, then remove from the bowl.

③ Fit the metal blade. Process the egg for a few seconds until roughly chopped. Add the courgette flesh and the ham, half the cheese and the parsley, and season with salt and pepper. Process for 3–4 seconds until combined.

④ Spoon the mixture into the courgette shells and sprinkle with the remaining cheese.

⑤ Bake in a preheated oven at 190°C/375°F/gas mark 5 for 30 minutes until golden.

Freezing tip: Freeze before baking. When required, thaw at room temperature for 3–4 hours, then bake as above.

PREPARATION AND COOKING TIME: 35 MINUTES

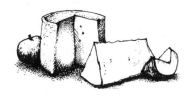

CHEESE AND WALNUT SABLES

—— SERVES 4 ——

✹ ✎ ❄ 3 MONTHS	METRIC	IMPERIAL	AMERICAN
Mature Cheddar or other strongly flavoured cheese	175 g	6 oz	6 oz
Walnuts	50 g	2 oz	½ cup
Plain (all-purpose) flour	175 g	6 oz	1½ cups
Butter or margarine, cut into pieces	175 g	6 oz	¾ cup
Egg, lightly beaten	1	1	1
A pinch of salt			

① Fit the grating disc. Grate the cheese, then remove from the bowl.

② Fit the metal blade. Process the walnuts for 5–6 seconds until chopped, then remove from the bowl.

③ Place the grated cheese, flour and butter or margarine in the bowl and process for 3–4 seconds until the mixture begins to hold together. Add the walnuts and process for 4–5 seconds until the mixture forms a ball around the blade.

④ Transfer to a lightly floured work surface and roll out to a 20 cm/8 in square.

⑤ Beat the egg with a little salt and brush over the pastry (paste). Cut the square in half, then cut crossways into 5 cm/2 in strips, then cut each strip into triangles.

⑥ Place on a lightly greased baking (cookie) sheet and bake in a preheated oven at 190°C/375°F/gas mark 5 for 8–10 minutes until golden brown. Sprinkle with salt while still hot and leave on the tray until just warm.

Freezing tip: Open-freeze until hard, then pack in freezer containers. When required, thaw at room temperature for 1 hour, then reheat at 190°C/375°F/gas mark 5 for 5 minutes before serving.

PREPARATION AND COOKING TIME: 20 MINUTES

SAUSAGE ROLLS
—— SERVES 4 ——

🌸 4 MONTHS	METRIC	IMPERIAL	AMERICAN
Slice of bread, roughly broken up	I	I	I
Dried mixed herbs	5 ml	I tsp	I tsp
Onion, quartered	I	I	I
Garlic clove, halved	I	I	I
Belly pork, trimmed and cut into chunks	225 g	8 oz	8 oz
French mustard	5 ml	I tsp	I tsp
Lemon juice	15 ml	I tbsp	I tbsp
Egg, lightly beaten	I	I	I
Frozen puff pastry (paste), thawed	450 g	I lb	I lb

① Fit the metal blade. Drop the bread and herbs through the feed tube with the motor running to make fine, even breadcrumbs. Remove from the bowl.

② Process the onion and garlic for 3–4 seconds until finely chopped, using the pulse button to prevent overprocessing.

③ Add the pork and process for 8–10 seconds until the meat is chopped and the mixture is even in texture and colour. Add the herbs and breadcrumbs, mustard and lemon juice and process briefly until blended. Pour the egg through the feed tube and process for a few seconds until blended.

④ Roll out the pastry on a lightly floured surface to a large rectangle and cut into 10 cm/4 in wide strips. Shape the sausagemeat down the centre of each strip, moisten the edges, then fold over and seal the pastry. Cut across into sausage rolls.

⑤ Place the rolls on a dampened baking (cookie) sheet and bake in a preheated oven at 200°C/400°F/gas mark 6 for about 25 minutes until golden brown and cooked through.

COOKING AND PREPARATION TIME: 40 MINUTES

BACON AND MUSHROOM QUICHE

—— SERVES 4–6 ——

✿ ⊕ ❋ 4 MONTHS	METRIC	IMPERIAL	AMERICAN
Self-raising (self-rising) flour	75 g	3 oz	¾ cup
Wholemeal flour	75 g	3 oz	¾ cup
A pinch of salt			
Butter or margarine, cut into pieces	50 g	2 oz	¼ cup
Lard (shortening), cut into pieces	25 g	1 oz	2 tbsp
Water	30 ml	2 tbsp	2 tbsp
Onion, quartered	1	1	1
Oil	15 ml	1 tbsp	1 tbsp
Streaky bacon, rinded	175 g	6 oz	6 oz
Mushrooms	175 g	6 oz	6 oz
Egg	1	1	1
Milk or single (light) cream	150 ml	¼ pt	⅔ cup
Salt and freshly ground black pepper			
Caraway seeds	5 ml	1 tsp	1 tsp

① Fit the metal blade. Process the flours, salt and fats for 7–8 seconds until the mixture looks like fine breadcrumbs. With the motor running, add the water through the feed tube until the pastry (paste) begins to form a ball around the blade.

② Remove the pastry from the bowl and roll out on a lightly floured surface, then use to line a greased 23 cm/9 in flan tin (pan). Prick all over the base with a fork.

③ Process the onion for 3–4 seconds until roughly chopped. Heat the oil and fry (sauté) for 5 minutes until soft.

④ Meanwhile, chop the bacon in the processor, then add to the onion and fry for 2–3 minutes.

⑤ Fit the slicing disc and slice the mushrooms. Sprinkle over the pastry base, then cover with the onion and bacon.

⑥ Beat together the egg and milk or cream, season and pour over the flan. Sprinkle with the caraway seeds.

⑦ Bake in a preheated oven at 200°C/400°F/gas mark 6 for 35–40 minutes until risen and golden brown.

PREPARATION AND COOKING TIME: 1 HOUR

LEEK AND STILTON FLAN

—— SERVES 4 ——

✿⊕❄ 3 MONTHS	METRIC	IMPERIAL	AMERICAN
Leeks	450 g	1 lb	1 lb
Butter or margarine	100 g	4 oz	½ cup
Plain (all-purpose) flour	75 g	3 oz	¾ cup
Wholemeal flour	75 g	3 oz	¾ cup
Stilton cheese	50 g	2 oz	2 oz
Water	30 ml	2 tbsp	2 tbsp
Streaky bacon, rinded	100 g	4 oz	4 oz
Single (light) cream	150 ml	¼ pt	⅔ cup
Made English mustard	2.5 ml	½ tsp	½ tsp
Dried mixed herbs	2.5 ml	½ tsp	½ tsp
Salt and freshly ground black pepper			
Green salad and new potatoes, to serve			

① Fit the slicing disc and slice the leeks.

② Heat 25 g/1 oz/2 tbsp of the butter or margarine and gently fry (sauté) the leeks for 15 minutes until soft.

③ Fit the metal blade. Process the flours, the remaining butter or margarine, and half the cheese for 10 seconds until the mixture resembles fine breadcrumbs. With the motor running, add the water through the feed tube until the mixture just begins to form a ball around the blade.

④ Transfer the dough to a lightly floured surface and press into a ball, then roll out and use to line a greased 23 cm/9 in flan dish. Spread the leeks over the base.

⑤ Process the bacon for 3–4 seconds until roughly chopped, then sprinkle over the leeks.

⑥ Mix together the cream, mustard, herbs, salt and pepper and pour the mixture over the leeks. Crumble over the remaining Stilton, then bake in a preheated oven at 200°C/400°F/gas mark 6 for 25–30 minutes until golden.

⑦ Serve hot with a green salad and new potatoes.

PREPARATION AND COOKING TIME: 1 HOUR

MEDITERRANEAN ONION AND PEPPER TART

—— SERVES 4 ——

⊛ ⤙ ⊕ ❋ 3 MONTHS	METRIC	IMPERIAL	AMERICAN
Strong hard cheese	50 g	2 oz	2 oz
Plain (all-purpose) flour	175 g	6 oz	1½ cups
A pinch of salt			
Butter or margarine	75 g	3 oz	⅓ cup
Water	30 ml	2 tbsp	2 tbsp
Onions	3	3	3
Red (bell) pepper, halved	1	1	1
Olive oil	15 ml	1 tbsp	1 tbsp
Eggs	2	2	2
Single (light) cream or milk	150 ml	¼ pt	⅔ cup
Chopped basil	15 ml	1 tbsp	1 tbsp
Salt and freshly ground black pepper			
Freshly grated Parmesan cheese	30 ml	2 tbsp	2 tbsp
Salad and ciabatta bread, to serve			

① Fit the grating disc and grate the cheese, then remove.

② Fix the metal blade. Process the flour, salt and butter or margarine until the mixture resembles fine breadcrumbs. With the motor running, add the water through the feed tube until the mixture forms a ball around the blade.

③ Turn out on to a lightly floured surface and press into a ball. Roll out and use to line a 20 cm/8 in flan dish.

④ Fit the slicing disc and slice the onions, then the pepper.

⑤ Heat the oil and gently fry (sauté) the onions for 5 minutes until soft. Add the pepper and fry for 5 minutes, then spread over the base of the flan.

⑥ Mix together the eggs, cream or milk, basil, salt and pepper, then pour the mixture into the flan case (pie shell). Sprinkle with the Parmesan cheese.

⑦ Bake in a preheated oven at 200°C/400°F/gas mark 6 for 30–40 minutes until well risen and golden brown.

⑧ Serve hot or cold with salad and ciabatta bread.

PREPARATION AND COOKING TIME: 1 HOUR

MEAT AND POULTRY MAIN COURSES

Once you get used to keeping your processor on the work surface, you'll get into the habit of using it to make all your cooking that much easier. Remember to trim meat well, as gristle and fat will process but will remain hard when cooked. For main courses, the processor makes a quick job of pastry (paste), crumbles and stuffings, as well as all your chopping, slicing or grating of vegetables, so almost everything you prepare is made quicker and easier.

When you are developing your own recipes, remember to think about the order in which you process foods so that you can avoid washing the bowl during preparation. For example, a few traces of chopped onions gives an added boost of flavour to a savoury pastry.

RICH BEEF AND MUSHROOM COBBLER

— SERVES 4 —

🍲 ⊕ ❄ 4 MONTHS	METRIC	IMPERIAL	AMERICAN
Onion, quartered	I	I	I
Garlic clove, halved	I	I	I
Oil	30 ml	2 tbsp	2 tbsp
Braising steak, cut into chunks	450 g	I lb	I lb
Mushrooms	100 g	4 oz	4 oz
Plain (all-purpose) flour	15 ml	I tbsp	I tbsp
Beef stock	450 ml	¾ pt	2 cups
Tomato purée (paste)	15 ml	I tbsp	I tbsp
Worcestershire sauce	5 ml	I tsp	I tsp
Juniper berries, crushed	4	4	4
Salt and freshly ground black pepper			
For the topping:			
Self-raising (self-rising) flour	225 g	8 oz	2 cups
Baking powder	5 ml	I tsp	I tsp
Butter or margarine	50 g	2 oz	¼ cup
Chopped parsley	30 ml	2 tbsp	2 tbsp
Milk	150 ml	¼ pt	⅔ cup

① Fit the metal blade. Process the onion and garlic for 5 seconds until evenly chopped.

② Heat the oil and gently fry (sauté) the onion and garlic for 5 minutes until softened but not browned.

③ Process the meat in two batches for 5–6 seconds until evenly chopped. Add to the meat and fry until browned.

④ Fit the slicing disc and slice the mushrooms, then add them to the meat and cook for 1 minute. Stir in the flour and mix well, then stir in the stock, tomato purée, Worcestershire sauce, juniper berries and salt and pepper to taste. Bring to the boil, leave to simmer gently for about 15 minutes or until the meat is tender, then pour into a casserole dish (Dutch oven).

⑤ Fit the metal blade and process the flour, baking powder, butter or margarine and parsley for about 3 seconds until the mixture resembles breadcrumbs. With the motor running, pour just enough of the milk through the feed tube until the mixture forms a soft dough.

⑥ Divide the dough into eight small balls and arrange around the edge of the casserole. Bake in a preheated oven at 200°C/400°F/gas mark 6 for 30 minutes until lightly browned.

PREPARATION AND COOKING TIME: 1 HOUR

HOME-MADE BEEFBURGERS

—— SERVES 4 ——

❀ 6 MONTHS	METRIC	IMPERIAL	AMERICAN
Slice of bread	I	I	I
Stewing steak, cut into chunks	450 g	I lb	I lb
Mushrooms	50 g	2 oz	2 oz
Thyme leaves	10 ml	2 tsp	2 tsp
French mustard	5 ml	I tsp	I tsp
Salt and freshly ground black pepper			
Egg, beaten	½	½	½
Sesame seed buns and coleslaw, to serve			

① Fit the metal blade. With the motor running, drop pieces of bread through the feed tube to make breadcrumbs. Remove from the bowl.

② Process the steak for 5–6 seconds until minced (ground). Add the mushrooms and process for 4–5 seconds until mixed. Add the breadcrumbs, thyme and mustard and season with salt and pepper. Process for 2 seconds. Add the egg and process for 2–3 seconds.

③ Tip the mixture on to a board and shape into burgers.

④ Fry (sauté) or grill (broil) for about 10 minutes until cooked through and browned, turning once. Serve hot in sesame seed buns with coleslaw.

COOKING AND PREPARATION TIME: 20 MINUTES

RAVIOLI WITH VEAL AND CELERY STUFFING

—— SERVES 4 ——

🍲 ❄ 2 MONTHS	METRIC	IMPERIAL	AMERICAN
For the pasta:			
Eggs	2	2	2
Strong plain (bread) flour	225 g	8 oz	2 cups
A pinch of salt			
Water	30 ml	2 tbsp	2 tbsp
For the stuffing:			
Onion, quartered	I	I	I
Garlic clove, halved	I	I	I
Oil	15 ml	I tbsp	I tbsp
Lean veal or chicken	175 g	6 oz	6 oz
Celery stick, quartered	I	I	I
Egg, beaten	½	½	½
Dried oregano	5 ml	I tsp	I tsp
Salt and freshly ground black pepper			
I quantity of Mushroom Sauce (see page 84)			
Freshly grated Parmesan cheese, to serve			

① Fit the metal blade and process the eggs for 10 seconds. With the motor running, add the flour and salt through the feed tube and process for a few seconds until mixed. Add the water and mix to a dough, adding a little more water if necessary to make it bind together, then process for 30 seconds to knead the dough. Cover with a damp cloth or clingfilm (plastic wrap) and leave to one side for 30 minutes.

② Process the onion and garlic for 8–10 seconds until finely chopped.

③ Heat the oil and gently fry (sauté) the onion and garlic for 5 minutes until softened but not browned.

④ Process the veal or chicken for 6–8 seconds until finely chopped. Add to the onions and fry until lightly browned. Process the celery for 5–6 seconds until finely chopped, then remove the meat from the heat and mix in the celery, egg, oregano and salt and pepper to taste.

⑤ Divide the dough in half and roll each piece out very thinly on a lightly floured surface to a 40 cm/16 in square.

⑥ Place 16 teaspoonfuls of the filling at 2.5 cm/1 in intervals on one sheet of dough. Moisten the dough in between the filling with a pastry (paste) brush, then carefully lay the second sheet of dough on top. Press together the joins, then cut into ravioli with a pastry wheel or sharp knife, making sure the edges are sealed.

⑦ Bring a large pan of salted water to a rolling boil. Add the ravioli, return the water to the boil, then cook for 8–10 minutes until the pasta is tender.

⑧ Meanwhile, make the Mushroom Sauce. Drain the ravioli well, then toss with the Mushroom Sauce and serve sprinkled with Parmesan cheese.

Freezing tip: Open-freeze the uncooked ravioli until hard, then pack in a polythene bag. When required, thaw at room temperature for 3–4 hours, then cook as above.

PREPARATION AND COOKING TIME: 40 MINUTES PLUS RESTING

SPAGHETTI BOLOGNESE

—— SERVES 4 ——

2 MONTHS	METRIC	IMPERIAL	AMERICAN
Onion, quartered	I	I	I
Garlic clove, halved	I	I	I
Olive oil	15 ml	I tbsp	I tbsp
Braising steak, cut into cubes	225 g	8 oz	8 oz
Mushrooms	50 g	2 oz	2 oz
Pigs' or lambs' liver	100 g	4 oz	4 oz
Dry sherry	15 ml	I tbsp	I tbsp
Plain (all-purpose) flour	15 ml	I tbsp	I tbsp
Can of tomatoes	400 g	14 oz	I large
Beef stock	450 ml	¾ pt	2 cups
Tomato purée (paste)	15 ml	I tbsp	I tbsp
Dried oregano	10 ml	2 tsp	2 tsp
Salt and freshly ground black pepper			
Spaghetti	225 g	8 oz	8 oz
Freshly grated Parmesan cheese	50 g	2 oz	½ cup

① Fit the metal blade and process the onion and garlic for 4–5 seconds until finely chopped.

② Heat the oil in a large saucepan and fry (sauté) the onion and garlic gently for 4 minutes until softened but not browned.

③ Process the steak for 7–8 minutes until evenly minced (ground). Add to the onions and fry until browned, stirring occasionally.

④ Fit the slicing disc and slice the mushrooms. Add to the steak and continue to cook for 2 minutes.

⑤ Fit the metal blade and process the liver for 4–5 seconds. Add to the pan with the sherry and cook for 1 minute. Add the flour and stir well. Add the tomatoes and their juice, the stock, tomato purée, oregano and salt and pepper to taste. Bring to the boil, then simmer gently for 20–30 minutes until thick, stirring occasionally.

⑥　Meanwhile, bring a large pan of salted water to the boil, add the spaghetti, return to the boil, then cook for about 10 minutes, as directed on the packet, until just tender. Drain well.

⑦　To serve, pour the sauce over the spaghetti and sprinkle with the Parmesan.

Freezing tip: Freeze the Bolognese Sauce to serve with freshly cooked spaghetti.

PREPARATION AND COOKING TIME: 45 MINUTES

MOUSSAKA

—— SERVES 4 ——

⊛ ⊕ ⌇ ❆ 3 MONTHS	METRIC	IMPERIAL	AMERICAN
Feta cheese	100 g	4 oz	1 cup
Aubergines (eggplants)	2	2	2
Salt and freshly ground black pepper			
Onion, quartered	1	1	1
Garlic clove, halved	1	1	1
Cold cooked lamb, cut into pieces	350 g	12 oz	3 cups
Chopped rosemary	2.5 ml	½ tsp	½ tsp
Chopped thyme	5 ml	1 tsp	1 tsp
Tomato purée (paste)	15 ml	1 tbsp	1 tbsp
Cornflour (cornstarch)	5 ml	1 tsp	1 tsp
Chicken or vegetable stock	150 ml	¼ pt	⅔ cup
Milk	450 ml	¾ pt	2 cups
Butter or margarine	25 g	1 oz	2 tbsp
Plain (all-purpose) flour	25 g	1 oz	¼ cup
Greek salad, to serve			

① Fit the grating disc and grate the cheese, then remove from the bowl.

② Fit the slicing disc and slice the aubergines. Spread on a plate and sprinkle generously with salt. Leave to stand while you prepare the rest of the dish.

③ Fit the metal blade and process the onion and garlic for 5 seconds until finely chopped. Add the lamb and process for 10 seconds until chopped. Add the herbs, tomato purée, cornflour, salt and pepper and process for 2–3 seconds to mix. Add the stock and mix again for 2–3 seconds. Transfer to an ovenproof casserole dish (Dutch oven).

④ Place the milk, butter or margarine and flour in the processor and process for 10 seconds until well blended.

⑤ Pour into a saucepan and bring to the boil, stirring continuously, then simmer for 2 minutes, stirring. Season generously with salt and pepper, then remove from the heat and stir in half the cheese.

⑥ Rinse the aubergines well in cold water, then drain and pat dry. Arrange on top of the casserole. Pour over the sauce and sprinkle with the remaining cheese.

⑦ Bake in a preheated oven at 200°C/400°F/gas mark 6 for 25–30 minutes until cooked through and golden brown.

PREPARATION AND COOKING TIME: 1 HOUR

STUFFED PORK FILLET

—— SERVES 4 ——

	METRIC	IMPERIAL	AMERICAN
Prunes, stoned (pitted)	9	9	9
Slice of bread	I	I	I
Butter or margarine, cut into pieces	100 g	4 oz	½ cup
Dried mixed herbs	5 ml	I tsp	I tsp
Salt and freshly ground black pepper			
Pork fillet	750 g	1½ lb	1½ lb
Rashers (slices) of streaky bacon, rinded	8	8	8
Rice or pasta, to serve			

① Fit the metal blade. Process the prunes for 4 seconds until roughly chopped. With the motor running, tear off pieces of bread and add them to the processor to make crumbs. Add 75 g/3 oz/⅓ cup of the butter or margarine, the herbs and salt and pepper and process for 4–5 seconds until well mixed.

② Cut the pork fillets almost in half lengthways, fill the centre with the stuffing, then fold the meat over.

③ Stretch the bacon rashers with the back of a knife, then wrap around the meat. Secure with cocktail sticks (toothpicks), then arrange in an flameproof dish and dot with the remaining butter. Grill (broil) under a hot grill (broiler) for 15 minutes, turning one or twice, until cooked through.

④ Serve with rice or pasta.

PREPARATION AND COOKING TIME: 30 MINUTES

CORNISH PASTIES

—— SERVES 6 ——

🥄 ❄ 6 MONTHS	METRIC	IMPERIAL	AMERICAN
Plain (all-purpose) flour	225 g	8 oz	2 cups
A pinch of salt			
Butter or margarine, cut into pieces	50 g	2 oz	¼ cup
Lard or vegetable fat (shortening)	50 g	2 oz	¼ cup
Water	90 ml	6 tbsp	6 tbsp
Onion, quartered	1	1	1
Potato, quartered	1	1	1
Carrot, quartered	1	1	1
Stewing steak, trimmed and cut into chunks	225 g	8 oz	8 oz
A few drops of Worcestershire sauce			
Egg, beaten	1	1	1

① Fit the metal blade. Process the flour, salt, butter or margarine and lard or vegetable fat for 10 seconds until the mixture resembles fine breadcrumbs. With the motor running, gradually add 45–60 ml/3–4 tbsp of the water through the feed tube until the mixture forms a ball around the blade.

② Divide the dough into six balls. Roll out on a lightly floured surface, then cut into six 15 cm/6 in circles.

③ Fit the metal blade and process the onion for 4–5 seconds until finely chopped. Remove from the bowl. Process the potato and carrot for 4–5 seconds until finely chopped. Remove from the bowl. Process the steak for about 8 seconds until minced (ground). Add the onion, carrot and potato. Mix the Worcestershire sauce with the remaining water and add to the bowl. Process for a further few seconds to mix. Divide the mixture into six.

④ Place a ball of mixture on each circle of pastry (paste), dampen the edges and lift over the filling, sealing and fluting the edges across the top. Brush with beaten egg.

⑤ Bake in a preheated oven at 190°C/375°F/gas mark 5 for 30–35 minutes. Serve hot or cold.

PREPARATION AND COOKING TIME: 50 MINUTES

FRESH HERB SAUSAGEMEAT ROLL

—— SERVES 4 ——

✿ ❄ 3 MONTHS	METRIC	IMPERIAL	AMERICAN
Slice of bread	I	I	I
A large bunch of parsley			
Sage leaves	2	2	2
Sprigs of thyme	2	2	2
Onion, quartered	I	I	I
Garlic clove, halved	I	I	I
Belly pork, cut into chunks	225 g	8 oz	8 oz
Egg	I	I	I
Lemon juice	10 ml	2 tbsp	2 tbsp
French mustard	2.5 ml	½ tsp	½ tsp
Salt and freshly ground black pepper			
Frozen puff pastry (paste), thawed	450 g	I lb	I lb
Green salad, to serve			

① Fit the metal blade. With the motor running, drop pieces of the bread through the feed tube to make breadcrumbs. Add the herbs and process for 3–4 seconds until finely chopped. Remove from the bowl.

② Process the onion and garlic for 4–5 seconds until finely chopped. Remove from the bowl.

③ Process the pork for 7–8 seconds until finely chopped. Add the onion and garlic, bread and herbs, egg, lemon juice and mustard, and season generously with salt and pepper. Process for 5–6 seconds until well combined.

④ Roll out the pastry on a lightly floured surface. Make the sausagemeat into a thick roll and place on the centre. Moisten the edges and fold over the filling. Turn over and place, seam-side down, on a dampened baking (cookie) sheet. Make two or three cuts on the top.

⑤ Bake in a preheated oven at 200°C/400°F/gas mark 6 for about 30 minutes until cooked through and golden. If the pastry begins to over-brown, cover with foil and continue to cook at 190°C/375°F/gas mark 5 until ready.

⑥ Serve hot with a green salad and tomato sauce.

PREPARATION TIME: 10 MINUTES

LAMB AND CORIANDER KEBABS
—— SERVES 4 ——

❄ 2 MONTHS	METRIC	IMPERIAL	AMERICAN
Slice of bread	1	1	1
Onion, quartered	1	1	1
Garlic clove, halved	1	1	1
Chopped coriander (cilantro)	15 ml	1 tbsp	1 tbsp
Chopped rosemary leaves	2.5 ml	½ tsp	½ tsp
Neck of lamb, boned and cut into chunks	750 g	1½ lb	1½ lb
Butter or margarine, cut into pieces	50 g	2 oz	¼ cup
Salt and freshly ground black pepper			
Small green (bell) pepper, cut into thick strips	1	1	1
Boiling water	600 ml	1 pt	2½ cups
Large tomatoes	2	2	2
Bay leaves	4	4	4
Olive oil	15 ml	1 tbsp	1 tbsp
Rice or hot pitta bread and salad, to serve			

① Fit the metal blade. With the motor running, drop in pieces of the bread to make crumbs. Remove from the bowl.

② Process the onion, garlic, coriander and rosemary for 4–5 seconds until finely chopped. Add the meat and process for 8–10 seconds until minced (ground). Add the breadcrumbs and butter or margarine and season generously. Process for 4 seconds until mixed. Divide the mixture into 12 and shape into balls, using floured hands. Chill for 30 minutes.

③ Place the pepper in a bowl, cover with the boiling water and leave to stand for 2 minutes. Drain and rinse. Cut the tomatoes into eight and remove the seeds.

④ Arrange the lamb, pepper, tomato and bay leaves alternately on four kebab skewers, then brush with oil. Grill (broil) for about 15 minutes until cooked through.

⑤ Serve with rice or hot pitta bread and salad.

PREPARATION AND COOKING TIME: 40 MINUTES PLUS CHILLING

LAMB CUTLETS WITH SOUBISE SAUCE

—— SERVES 4 ——

❄ 2 MONTHS	METRIC	IMPERIAL	AMERICAN
Slices of bread	4	4	4
Onions or shallots, quartered	225 g	8 oz	8 oz
Water	150 ml	¼ pt	⅔ cup
Milk	450 ml	¾ pt	2 cups
Plain (all-purpose) flour	25 g	1 oz	¼ cup
Butter or margarine	25 g	1 oz	2 tbsp
Salt and freshly ground black pepper			
Single (light) cream	15 ml	1 tbsp	1 tbsp
Egg	1	1	1
Lamb cutlets	8	8	8
Oil	15 ml	1 tbsp	1 tbsp
Fresh pasta, to serve			

① Fit the metal blade. With the motor running, drop pieces of the bread through the feed tube to make breadcrumbs. Remove from the bowl.

② Process the onions for 5 seconds until finely chopped. Turn into a small pan, add the water, bring to the boil, then simmer gently for 10 minutes until soft.

③ Process the milk, flour and butter or margarine for 10 seconds until well blended. Pour into a pan and bring to the boil, stirring continuously, then simmer gently for 2 minutes, stirring. Season.

④ Pour the onion and water into the processor and process for 15 seconds to a smooth purée. Add the sauce and cream and process for 4–5 seconds to mix. Return to the pan and reheat gently, if necessary, when ready to serve.

⑤ Beat the egg with 5 ml/1 tsp water and some salt and pepper. Dip each cutlet in the egg. Heat the oil in a frying pan (skillet) and fry (sauté) the cutlets for 10 minutes until tender and lightly browned, turning once.

⑥ Spoon the soubise sauce over the cutlets and serve with freshly cooked pasta.

PREPARATION AND COOKING TIME: 30 MINUTES

POTATO PASTRY ROLL

—— SERVES 4 ——

❅ 3 MONTHS	METRIC	IMPERIAL	AMERICAN
Plain (all-purpose) flour	175 g	6 oz	1½ cups
Butter or margarine, cut into pieces	75 g	3 oz	⅓ cup
Cold mashed potato	175 g	6 oz	6 oz
Slices of wholemeal or white bread	2	2	2
Sage leaves	2	2	2
Onion, quartered	1	1	1
Red (bell) pepper	1	1	1
Garlic clove, halved	1	1	1
Belly pork, trimmed, rinded and cut into large chunks	225 g	8 oz	8 oz
Eating (dessert) apple, peeled, cored and quartered	1	1	1
Grated rind and juice of 1 small lemon			
French mustard	5 ml	1 tsp	1 tsp
Chopped parsley	15 ml	1 tbsp	1 tbsp
Salt and freshly ground black pepper			
Egg, beaten	1	1	1
Seasonal vegetables or salad, to serve			

① Fit the metal blade. Process the flour and butter or margarine for 6–7 seconds until the mixture resembles breadcrumbs. Add the mashed potato and process for 5–6 seconds until the mixture forms a ball around the blade. Remove from the bowl, press into a ball, cover with clingfilm (plastic wrap) and chill while preparing the filling.

② With the motor running, drop pieces of the bread into the processor to make breadcrumbs. Add the sage leaves and process until chopped. Remove from the bowl.

③ Process the onion, pepper and garlic for 6–8 seconds until finely chopped. Remove from the bowl.

④ Process the pork for 7–8 seconds until evenly chopped. Add the apple and process for 2–3 seconds, then add the breadcrumbs, onion mixture and all the remaining ingredients except the egg and process for 7–8 seconds until well combined.

⑤ Roll out the pastry (paste) on a lightly floured surface to a 25 × 20 cm/10 × 8 in rectangle about 5 mm/¼ in thick. Place the meat mixture along the centre, dampen the edges of the pastry with water, then fold the long sides over to the middle and pinch together. Fold in and seal the short ends.

⑥ Place seam-side down on a greased baking (cookie) sheet and pinch the edges to make a scalloped edge. Glaze generously with beaten egg and bake in a preheated oven at 190°C/375°F/gas mark 5 for 30–40 minutes until cooked through and golden brown.

⑦ Serve hot with seasonal vegetables or cold as a picnic dish or with salad.

PREPARATION AND COOKING TIME: 1 HOUR

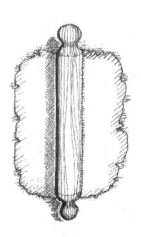

PORK-STUFFED MUSHROOMS

—— SERVES 4 ——

🍲 ❄ 3 MONTHS	METRIC	IMPERIAL	AMERICAN
Onion, quartered	I	I	I
Garlic clove, halved	I	I	I
Slice of bread	I	I	I
Sage leaves	I–2	I–2	I–2
Thyme leaves	5 ml	I tsp	I tsp
Belly pork, cut into chunks	225 g	8 oz	8 oz
Egg	I	I	I
Lemon juice	I5 ml	I tbsp	I tbsp
French mustard	5 ml	I tsp	I tsp
Large flat mushrooms, stalks removed and reserved	8	8	8
Dry sherry	30 ml	2 tbsp	2 tbsp
Rashers (slices) of streaky bacon, rinded	2	2	2

① Fit the metal blade. Process the onion and garlic for 4–5 seconds until evenly chopped. Remove from the bowl.

② With the motor running, drop pieces of bread through the feed tube to make breadcrumbs. Add the herbs and process for 2 seconds until chopped. Remove from the bowl.

③ Process the pork for 8–10 seconds until the mixture is evenly textured and coloured. Add the onion and garlic and the breadcrumb mixture and process for 3 seconds until mixed. Add the egg, lemon juice, mustard and mushroom stalks and process for 3 seconds.

④ Place the mushrooms in a single layer in a shallow ovenproof dish. Divide the stuffing mixture between them and press down gently into the mushroom caps. Pour the sherry around.

⑤ Process the bacon for 3 seconds until finely chopped, then sprinkle on top of the mushrooms.

⑥ Cover with foil and bake in a preheated oven at 190°C/375°F/gas mark 5 for 35 minutes.

PREPARATION AND COOKING TIME: 45 MINUTES

CHICKEN-STUFFED PANCAKES

—— SERVES 4 ——

✎	METRIC	IMPERIAL	AMERICAN
Plain (all-purpose) flour	150 g	5 oz	1¼ cups
Egg	1	1	1
Milk	300 ml	½ pt	1¼ cups
A pinch of salt			
Oil	30 ml	2 tbsp	2 tbsp
Mushrooms	100 g	4 oz	4 oz
Butter or margarine	75 g	3 oz	⅓ cup
Chicken stock	300 ml	½ pt	1¼ cups
Chopped parsley	15 ml	1 tbsp	1 tbsp
Salt and freshly ground black pepper			
Cooked chicken	225 g	8 oz	2 cups

① Fit the metal blade. Process 100 g/4 oz/1 cup of the flour with the egg, milk and salt for 10 seconds until smooth.

② Heat a little of the oil in a frying pan (skillet) and pour in enough of the batter to cover the base of the pan. Cook the pancake until golden on the underside, then turn and cook the other side. Repeat to make eight pancakes in all.

③ Rinse the bowl and refit the metal blade. Process the mushrooms until roughly chopped.

④ Melt half the butter or margarine and fry (sauté) the mushrooms for a few minutes until soft. Stir in the flour and cook for 1 minute, then gradually add the stock. Bring to the boil, stirring continuously, then add the parsley and season to taste with salt and pepper.

⑤ Process the chicken until roughly chopped, then stir into the sauce. Allow to cool.

⑥ Divide the chicken and sauce between the pancakes, then fold over the edges to make square parcels. Place in a large shallow dish, folded sides down, and dot the remaining butter or margarine over the top.

⑦ Cover with foil and cook in a preheated oven at 200°C/400°F/gas mark 6 for 15–20 minutes until hot and golden.

PREPARATION AND COOKING TIME: 40 MINUTES

CHICKEN AND PARMA HAM CANNELLONI

—— SERVES 4 ——

🐟 ⊛ ❄ 2 MONTHS	METRIC	IMPERIAL	AMERICAN
Onion, quartered	I	I	I
Cooked chicken, cut into chunks	225 g	8 oz	2 cups
Mushrooms	50 g	2 oz	2 oz
Parma ham	50 g	2 oz	2 oz
Dried oregano	5 ml	I tsp	I tsp
Salt and freshly ground black pepper			
Egg	I	I	I
Cannelloni tubes	16	16	16
Butter or margarine	75 g	3 oz	⅓ cup
Plain (all-purpose) flour	75 g	3 oz	¾ cup
Milk	900 ml	1½ pts	3½ cups
Grated nutmeg	2.5 ml	½ tsp	½ tsp
Parmesan cheese	50 g	2 oz	2 oz
Green salad, to serve			

① Fit the metal blade. Process the onion, chicken, mushrooms and ham separately for a few seconds each. Mix in the oregano and season to taste with salt and pepper.

② Lightly beat the egg, then use to bind the stuffing mixture.

③ Stuff the cannelloni tubes with the mixture, then arrange in a shallow ovenproof dish in one layer.

④ Process the butter or margarine, the flour and half the milk for 8 seconds until blended. Pour into a pan, add the remaining milk and the nutmeg, then season and bring to the boil, stirring continuously. Simmer gently until the sauce thickens, then pour over the cannelloni.

⑤ Fit the grating disc and grate the cheese. Sprinkle over the sauce.

⑥ Bake in a preheated oven at 180°C/350°F/gas mark 4 for 40 minutes until hot and golden on top.

⑦ Serve hot with a green salad.

PREPARATION AND COOKING TIME: 50 MINUTES

CHICKEN ROULADE

—— SERVES 4 ——

⊛ ⟲	METRIC	IMPERIAL	AMERICAN
Cheddar cheese	25 g	I oz	I oz
Plain (all-purpose) flour	50 g	2 oz	½ cup
Butter or margarine	50 g	2 oz	¼ cup
Milk	300 ml	½ pt	I ¼ cups
Salt and freshly ground black pepper			
Eggs, separated	2	2	2
Cooked chicken	175 g	6 oz	I ½ cups
Hard-boiled (hard-cooked) egg, quartered	I	I	I
Single (light) cream	30 ml	2 tbsp	2 tbsp
Green salad, to serve			

① Fit the grating disc and grate the cheese, then remove from the bowl.

② Fit the metal blade. Process the flour, butter or margarine and milk for 10 seconds until well blended.

③ Pour into a saucepan and bring to the boil, stirring, then simmer until the sauce thickens. Season generously.

④ Reserve 30 ml/2 tbsp of the sauce in a small pan, then pour the rest back into the processor. Add the egg yolks and process for 5–6 seconds until well blended. Whisk the egg whites until stiff, then fold into the sauce.

⑤ Grease and line a Swiss roll tin (jelly roll pan) and pour the roulade into the tin. Bake in a preheated oven at 180°C/350°F/gas mark 4 for 15–20 minutes until well risen and golden brown. Turn out of the tin on to a sheet of greaseproof (waxed) paper.

⑥ Process the chicken until finely chopped. Add the hard-boiled egg and process for 2–3 seconds. Transfer to the reserved sauce in the pan and add the cream. Spread over the roulade and roll up, using the paper to help. Place on an ovenproof serving dish, sprinkle with the cheese and return to the oven for 5–10 minutes.

⑦ Serve hot with a green salad.

PREPARATION AND COOKING TIME: 30 MINUTES

CHICKEN AND PORK LAYER PIE

—— SERVES 4 ——

🌱 ❄ 2 MONTHS	METRIC	IMPERIAL	AMERICAN
Plain (all-purpose) flour	275 g	10 oz	2½ cups
A pinch of salt			
Lard or vegetable fat (shortening), cut into pieces	40 g	1½ oz	3 tbsp
Butter or margarine, cut into pieces	75 g	3 oz	⅓ cup
Eggs, beaten	2	2	2
Lean pork, roughly cubed	350 g	12 oz	12 oz
Onion, quartered	1	1	1
Belly pork, rinded and cut into chunks	100 g	4 oz	4 oz
Dried marjoram	2.5 ml	½ tsp	½ tsp
Salt and freshly ground black pepper			
Cooked chicken, cut into strips	100 g	4 oz	1 cup

① Fit the metal blade and process the flour, salt, lard or vegetable fat and butter or margarine until the mixture resembles breadcrumbs. Reserve half an egg for glazing, then add the remainder to the processor and process for 25 seconds until the mixture forms a ball around the blade. Remove from the bowl, wrap in clingfilm (plastic wrap) and chill until required.

② Process the lean pork in two batches in short bursts until finely and evenly chopped, then remove from the bowl.

③ Process the onion for 4–5 seconds until chopped, then remove from the bowl and process the belly pork for 7–8 seconds until chopped. Add the chopped onion and marjoram and season generously with salt and pepper.

④ Grease a 450 g/1 lb loaf tin (pan). Fold a long strip of greaseproof (waxed) paper and place along the length of the tin, sticking out at either end to help you lift out the finished pie.

⑤ Roll out two-thirds of the pastry (paste) on a lightly
floured surface and use to line the tin. Fill with half the
lean pork, then half the belly pork mixture. Arrange the
chicken strips on top, then finish with second layers of
the two pork mixtures. Roll out the remaining dough to
make a lid, and seal on to the pie, crimping the edges.
Decorate with pastry leaves and glaze well with beaten
egg. Cut two steam vents on the top.

⑥ Bake in a preheated oven at 200°C/400°F/gas mark 6 for
45 minutes. Lower the oven temperature to 170°C/325°F/
gas mark 3 for a further 45 minutes. Allow to cool in the
tin.

⑦ Serve cold, cut into slices.

Freezing tip: Cool completely, then slice thickly. Interleaf
the slices with greaseproof paper, overwrap, then freeze.
When required, thaw at room temperature for 3–4 hours.

PREPARATION AND COOKING TIME: 2 HOURS

BRAISED LEMON CHICKEN

—— SERVES 4 ——

⊕ ◡ ❀ 4 MONTHS	METRIC	IMPERIAL	AMERICAN
Celery stick	I	I	I
Onion, quartered	I	I	I
Large cooking (tart) apple, peeled, cored and quartered	I	I	I
Chicken portions	4	4	4
Butter or margarine, cut into pieces	50 g	2 oz	¼ cup
French mustard	5 ml	I tsp	I tsp
Dried mixed herbs	5 ml	I tsp	I tsp
Salt and freshly ground black pepper			
Lemon	I	I	I
Chicken stock	300 ml	½ pt	I ¼ cups

① Fit the slicing disc and slice the celery, onion and apple. Place all the fruit and vegetables in the base of a shallow ovenproof dish. Place the chicken portions on top.

② Fit the metal blade. Process the butter or margarine, mustard, herbs, salt and pepper for 6–7 seconds until soft.

③ Halve the lemon. Slice one half and grate the rind and squeeze the juice of the other half. Add the lemon rind and juice to the butter mixture and process for 6–7 seconds until blended.

④ Spread the butter liberally over the chicken portions, pour in the stock and cover the dish.

⑤ Bake in a preheated oven at 200°C/400°F/gas mark 6 for 35–40 minutes until the chicken is tender and the juices run clear. Remove the lid and bake for a further 10 minutes until browned.

PREPARATION AND COOKING TIME: 50 MINUTES

VEGETARIAN AND SEAFOOD DISHES

For vegetarians, or those who are just increasing the vegetable meals in their diet, these recipes offer an interesting selection. They do include cheeses and dairy products, so you may need to adjust ingredients to suit your own dietary style.

Be careful when processing fish as the soft flesh breaks up easily and only needs a few seconds in the processor; it is best to use the pulse button to avoid overprocessing.

As a simple dish, make a white sauce (see page 83) and add some cooked and flaked white fish, a few prawns (shrimp) and a chopped hard-boiled (hard-cooked) egg. Spoon into a casserole dish (Dutch oven), sprinkle with breadcrumbs and dot with butter. Bake in a preheated oven at 200°C/400°F/gas mark 6 for about 20 minutes until hot and golden. The same filling can be topped with puff pastry (paste) for a tasty pie.

NUT AND BEAN LOAF

—— SERVES 4 ——

✪ ✎ ❋ 3 MONTHS	METRIC	IMPERIAL	AMERICAN
Cheddar or other strong cheese	100 g	4 oz	4 oz
Slices of bread	4	4	4
Hazelnuts (filberts)	50 g	2 oz	½ cup
Peanuts	50 g	2 oz	½ cup
Onion, quartered	1	1	1
Can of kidney beans, drained	400 g	14 oz	1 large
Oil	15 ml	1 tbsp	1 tbsp
Carrots	225 g	8 oz	8 oz
Chopped thyme	10 ml	2 tsp	2 tsp
Dried mixed herbs	5 ml	1 tsp	1 tsp
Caraway seeds	½ tsp	½ tsp	½ tsp
Salt and freshly ground black pepper			
Egg, lightly beaten	1	1	1
Tomato and Lentil Sauce (see page 85) and a selection of vegetables, to serve			

① Fit the grating disc and grate the cheese, then remove it from the bowl.

② Fit the metal blade. With the motor running, drop pieces of the bread through the feed tube to make breadcrumbs. Remove from the bowl. Process the nuts for 10 seconds until coarsely chopped, then remove from the bowl. Process the onion for 4 seconds until finely chopped, then remove. Process the kidney beans for 5 seconds, then remove.

③ Heat the oil and fry (sauté) the onion for 5 minutes until softened but not browned.

④ Fit the grating disc and grate the carrots.

⑤ Mix the onions with the processed ingredients, then stir in the mixed herbs and caraway seeds and season with salt and pepper. Bind together with the beaten egg and turn into a greased 450 g/1 lb loaf tin (pan) and press down well. Cover with foil and bake in a preheated oven at 190°C/375°F/gas mark 5 for 45 minutes.

⑥ Serve hot, cut into slices, with Tomato and Lentil Sauce and a selection of vegetables.

PREPARATION AND COOKING TIME: 1 HOUR

PLAICE ENVELOPES
—— SERVES 4 ——

🐟	METRIC	IMPERIAL	AMERICAN
Onion, quartered	I	I	I
Mushrooms	50 g	2 oz	2 oz
Butter or margarine, cut into pieces	50 g	2 oz	2 oz
Salt and freshly ground black pepper			
Plaice fillets	4	4	4
Tomatoes, sliced	2	2	2
Rice or green salad, to serve			

① Fit the metal blade. Process the onion for 5 seconds until finely chopped.

② Add the mushrooms and butter or margarine and season generously with salt and pepper. Process for 6 seconds until well blended.

③ Make a cut lengthways down the middle of each fillet through the flesh but not through the skin, then ease the flesh away from the skin to create a cavity.

④ Divide the filling between the fillets, then fold the flesh over the filling and arrange in a shallow ovenproof dish with the tomato slices on top.

⑤ Bake in a preheated oven at 200°C/400°F/gas mark 6 for 15–20 minutes until cooked through.

⑥ Serve hot with rice or a green salad.

PREPARATION AND COOKING TIME: 30 MINUTES

SMOKED CHEESE AND VEGETABLE PIE
—— SERVES 4 ——

⊕ ⊛ 🗞 ❀ 2 MONTHS	METRIC	IMPERIAL	AMERICAN
Onion, quartered	I	I	I
Leeks	2	2	2
Oil	30 ml	2 tbsp	2 tbsp
Potato	I	I	I
Carrots	4	4	4
Can of sweetcorn (corn), drained	175 g	6 oz	I small
Smoked cheese	75 g	3 oz	3 oz
Eggs	2	2	2
Milk	90 ml	6 tbsp	6 tbsp
Salt and freshly ground black pepper			
Self-raising (self-rising) flour	100 g	4 oz	I cup
Wholemeal flour	100 g	4 oz	I cup
Butter or margarine	100 g	4 oz	½ cup
Dried mixed herbs	5 ml	I tsp	I tsp
Water	60 ml	4 tbsp	4 tbsp
Noodles or green salad, to serve			

① Fit the slicing disc and slice the onion, then the leeks.

② Heat the oil and gently fry (sauté) the onion and leeks for 5 minutes until softened but not browned.

③ Cut the potato to fit the feed tube, then slice it. Arrange on the base of a shallow pie dish.

④ Fit the grating disc and grate the carrots, then arrange on top of the potatoes. Sprinkle with the sweetcorn, followed by the onion and leek mixture.

⑤ Fit the slicing disc and slice the cheese. Arrange on top of the vegetables. Beat one egg with the milk, season generously with salt and pepper, then pour over the vegetables.

⑥ Fit the metal blade and process the flours, butter or margarine and mixed herbs for 5–7 seconds until the mixture resembles breadcrumbs. With the motor running, gradually add the water and process until the mixture just forms a ball around the blade.

⑦ Roll out the pastry (paste) on a lightly floured surface, then fit on top of the pie dish. Trim the edges and decorate with pastry leaves. Brush with beaten egg to glaze, then bake in a preheated oven at 220°C/425°F/gas mark 7 for 20 minutes until the pastry is golden brown. Reduce the oven temperature to 190°/C375°F/gas mark 5 and cook for a further 20–25 minutes.

⑧ Serve hot with noodles or a green salad.

PREPARATION AND COOKING TIME: 1 HOUR

PRAWN-STUFFED EGGS

—— SERVES 4 ——

	METRIC	IMPERIAL	AMERICAN
Lettuce leaves	8	8	8
Cucumber	½	½	½
Tomatoes	2	2	2
Prawns (shrimp)	50 g	2 oz	2 oz
Hard-boiled (hard-cooked) eggs	4	4	4
Cream cheese	100 g	4 oz	½ cup
Butter, cut into pieces	50 g	2 oz	¼ cup
A few drops of Tabasco sauce			
Salt and freshly ground black pepper			

① Arrange the lettuce leaves on a serving plate. Fit the slicing disc and slice the cucumber and tomatoes, then arrange on top of the lettuce.

② Fit the metal blade. Reserve eight prawns for decoration. Process the remainder for 6–7 seconds until chopped.

③ Cut the eggs in half lengthways and remove the yolks. Add the yolks to the processor with the cream cheese, butter and Tabasco sauce, and season to taste with salt and pepper. Process for 7–8 seconds until well blended.

④ Pipe or spoon the mixture into the halved eggs, then arrange on top of the salad and garnish with the reserved prawns.

PREPARATION TIME: 10 MINUTES

INDIVIDUAL WHOLEMEAL PIZZAS

—— SERVES 4 ——

🍃 ⊛ ⊕ ❄ 3 MONTHS	METRIC	IMPERIAL	AMERICAN
Strong plain (bread) flour	100 g	4 oz	1 cup
Wholemeal flour	100 g	4 oz	1 cup
Sachet of fast-action dried yeast	1	1	1
A pinch of salt			
A pinch of sugar			
Butter or margarine	25 g	1 oz	2 tbsp
Milk	75 ml	5 tbsp	5 tbsp
Boiling water	45 ml	3 tbsp	3 tbsp
Olive oil	60 ml	4 tbsp	4 tbsp
Passata (sieved tomatoes)	250 ml	8 fl oz	1 cup
Onion, quartered	1	1	1
Red (bell) pepper	1	1	1
Mozzarella cheese	225 g	8 oz	8 oz
Dried oregano	10 ml	2 tsp	2 tsp
Salt and freshly ground black pepper			
Large tomatoes	2	2	2

① Fit the metal blade and process the flours, yeast, salt and sugar for a few seconds to mix. Add the butter or margarine and process for 3 seconds to combine. Mix the milk with the boiling water. With the motor running, pour the mixture in through the feed tube until the mixture forms a dough, then continue to process for a further 20 seconds to knead the dough.

② Place the dough in an oiled bowl, cover with oiled clingfilm (plastic wrap) and leave to rise for 1 hour until doubled in size.

③ Turn the dough on to a lightly floured surface and divide into four. Shape each piece into a ball, press or roll out into 20 cm/8 in circles and place on greased baking (cookie) sheets. Brush generously with olive oil and spoon over the passata.

④ Process the onion for 4 seconds until chopped, then sprinkle over the pizzas. Process the pepper for about 3–4 seconds until chopped, then sprinkle over the pizzas.

⑤   Fit the grating disc and grate the cheese, then sprinkle over the pizzas with the oregano and seasoning.

⑥   Fit the slicing disc, slice the tomatoes and arrange on top. Bake in a preheated oven at 200°C/400°F/gas mark 6 for 20–25 minutes until golden.

Freezing tip: Open-freeze the uncooked pizzas, then wrap and freeze. Cook from frozen at 200°C/400°F/gas mark 6 for 45 minutes.

PREPARATION AND COOKING TIME: 45 MINUTES PLUS RISING

FISH CAKES
—— SERVES 4 ——

	METRIC	IMPERIAL	AMERICAN
Slices of bread	2	2	2
A few sprigs of parsley			
White fish, such as cod or haddock	450 g	1 lb	1 lb
Milk	150 ml	¼ pt	⅔ cup
Cooked potatoes, mashed	450 g	1 lb	1 lb
A pinch of grated nutmeg			
Salt and freshly ground black pepper			
Egg, beaten	1	1	1
A little oil			

①   Fit the metal blade. With the motor running, drop pieces of the bread through the feed tube to make breadcrumbs. Remove from the bowl. Process the parsley for a few seconds until finely chopped, then remove from the bowl.

②   Poach the fish in the milk for 8–10 minutes until tender. Remove any remaining skin or bones, then process the fish and liquor for a few seconds to break up the fish.

③   Mix the fish with the mashed potatoes, parsley, nutmeg and seasoning. Shape into balls and flatten slightly. Coat in the egg and breadcrumbs and chill for 30 minutes.

④   Heat the oil and shallow-fry the fish cakes for 3–5 minutes each side until cooked and golden brown.

PREPARATION AND COOKING TIME: 25 MINUTES PLUS CHILLING

PRAWN AND RICE RING

—— SERVES 4 ——

	METRIC	IMPERIAL	AMERICAN
Long-grain rice	400 g	14 oz	1¾ cups
Lemon juice	10 ml	2 tsp	2 tsp
Butter or margarine, cut into pieces	15 g	½ oz	1 tbsp
Celery sticks, cut into chunks	4	4	4
Red (bell) pepper, quartered	1	1	1
Oil	15 ml	1 tbsp	1 tbsp
Beansprouts	75 g	3 oz	3 oz
Prawns (shrimp)	175 g	6 oz	6 oz
Dry sherry	15 ml	1 tbsp	1 tbsp
Can of tomatoes, drained	200 g	7 oz	1 small
Salt and freshly ground black pepper			

① Cook the long-grain rice with the lemon juice in a large pan of boiling salted water for 12 minutes. Drain well, then rinse with plenty of hot water. Press into a lightly oiled 900 ml/1½ pt/3¾ cup ring mould and dot with the butter or margarine.

② Bake in a preheated oven at 200°C/400°F/gas mark 6 for 10–15 minutes.

③ Meanwhile, fit the metal blade and process the celery for 5 seconds until finely chopped. Remove from the bowl. Process the pepper for 5 seconds until chopped.

④ Heat the oil and stir-fry the celery for a few minutes until soft. Add half the pepper and stir-fry for 3 minutes. Add the beansprouts and prawns and stir-fry for 2 minutes. Add the sherry.

⑤ Process the remaining pepper with the tomatoes until smooth. Pour into the pan and cook for 5 minutes. Season with salt and pepper.

⑥ To turn out the rice ring, loosen the edges with a knife, cover the ring with a flat plate and turn upside down. Shake sharply so the ring falls on to the plate, then remove the mould. Spoon the sauce into the centre of the ring and serve at once.

PREPARATION AND COOKING TIME: 35 MINUTES

SEAFOOD SOUFFLÉ

—— SERVES 4 ——

⊛ ⊚	METRIC	IMPERIAL	AMERICAN
Cheddar cheese	50 g	2 oz	2 oz
Slice of bread	I	I	I
Haddock fillet, skinned	225 g	8 oz	8 oz
Milk	150 ml	¼ pt	⅔ cup
Butter or margarine	15 g	½ oz	I tbsp
Plain (all-purpose) flour	15 ml	I tbsp	I tbsp
Salt and freshly ground black pepper			
Eggs, separated	3	3	3
Prawns (shrimp)	100 g	4 oz	4 oz

① Fit the grating disc and grate the cheese. Remove from the bowl and set aside.

② Fit the metal blade. With the motor running, drop pieces of the bread through the feed tube to make breadcrumbs. Remove from the bowl.

③ Place the haddock and milk in a pan and bring to the boil, then simmer gently for about 8 minutes until tender. Remove the fish, flake the flesh and set aside.

④ Strain the milk into the processor, add the butter or margarine and flour and process for 4–5 seconds until smooth. Season with salt and pepper, then return to the pan and bring to the boil, stirring until thick. Return to the processor, add the egg yolks and process for 4–5 seconds until blended.

⑤ Add the haddock and prawns to the sauce. Whisk the egg whites until stiff, then fold into the sauce. Turn into a well buttered 18 cm/7 in soufflé dish and sprinkle with the breadcrumbs and cheese.

⑥ Bake in a preheated oven at 200°C/400°F/gas mark 6 for 30–35 minutes until well risen and brown. Serve at once.

PREPARATION AND COOKING TIME: 50 MINUTES

VEGETABLE DISHES

A food processor makes light work of almost every kind of vegetable preparation. However, cooked potatoes do not mash well in a processor as they tend to become overworked in just a few seconds.

Fresh vegetables can be bought cheaply at the height of their season, then cooked and puréed, or chopped and sliced and blanched, ready to freeze for use later in the year.

BRAISED RED CABBAGE

—— SERVES 4 ——

⊕ ❄ 6 MONTHS	METRIC	IMPERIAL	AMERICAN
Onion, quartered	I	I	I
Butter or margarine	25 g	I oz	2 tbsp
Cooking (tart) apple, peeled, cored and quartered	I	I	I
Medium red cabbage, trimmed	I	I	I
White wine vinegar	30 ml	2 tbsp	2 tbsp
Water	45 ml	3 tbsp	3 tbsp
Sugar	I0 ml	2 tsp	2 tsp
Salt and freshly ground black pepper			

① Fit the slicing disc and slice the onion.

② Melt the butter or margarine in a saucepan and gently fry (sauté) the onion for a few minutes until softened.

③ Slice the apple and add to the onion and leave over a gentle heat. Meanwhile, slice the cabbage in batches as necessary. Remove from the bowl.

④ Arrange the apple and onion mixture over the base of a casserole dish (Dutch oven), then add the cabbage.

⑤ Mix the wine vinegar, water and sugar, and season with salt and pepper. Pour over the cabbage and cover the dish.

⑥ Cook in a preheated oven at 160°C/325°F/gas mark 3 for 1½ hours until tender.

PREPARATION AND COOKING TIME: 2 HOURS

ROSTI NEST

—— SERVES 4 ——

⊛	METRIC	IMPERIAL	AMERICAN
Potatoes, peeled	450 g	I lb	I lb
Olive oil	30 ml	2 tbsp	2 tbsp
Salt and freshly ground black pepper			
Eggs	4	4	4

① Cook the potatoes in boiling salted water for about 5 minutes; the potatoes should still be hard. Drain and rinse under cold running water.

② Fit the grating disc and grate the potatoes. Season well with salt and pepper.

③ Heat the oil in a large frying pan (skillet) and spread the grated potato over the pan. Cook gently for about 10 minutes until the potato is softening and the bottom is golden brown but not crisp.

④ Slide the potato out on to a plate, then invert it back into the pan and press four hollows in the mixture.

⑤ Break the eggs into the hollows, cover and cook for about 5 minutes until the base is golden brown and the eggs are cooked to your liking.

⑥ Serve hot, cut into wedges, with grilled meats or with salad as a lunch dish.

PREPARATION AND COOKING TIME: 25 MINUTES

SAUTÉ POTATOES WITH PEPPERS

—— SERVES 4 ——

	METRIC	IMPERIAL	AMERICAN
Green (bell) pepper, quartered	I	I	I
Onion, quartered	I	I	I
Olive oil	45 ml	3 tbsp	3 tbsp
Potatoes	450 g	I lb	I lb
Salt and freshly ground black pepper			

① Fit the metal blade and process the pepper and onion for 4–5 seconds until finely chopped.

② Heat the oil in a frying pan (skillet) and fry (sauté) the pepper and onion for about 5 minutes until softened but not browned.

③ Fit the slicing disc and thinly slice the potatoes.

④ Remove the pepper and onion from the pan and arrange the potato slices around the pan, overlapping slightly. Cover and cook for 7–8 minutes until browned underneath and soft on top.

⑤ Turn the potatoes over and sprinkle with the pepper and onion mixture. Season well with salt and pepper and cook for a further 5 minutes until cooked through and golden brown on the base.

PREPARATION AND COOKING TIME: 25 MINUTES

LEEKS IN SAGE BUTTER
—— SERVES 4 ——

	METRIC	IMPERIAL	AMERICAN
Leeks	450 g	1 lb	1 lb
Butter or margarine	50 g	2 oz	¼ cup
Chopped sage	5 ml	1 tsp	1 tsp
Dry white wine	30 ml	2 tbsp	2 tbsp
Salt and freshly ground black pepper			

① Fit the slicing disc and slice the leeks.

② Melt the butter or margarine in a large saucepan, add the leeks and toss well. Add the sage, using a little more to taste if you like a strong herb flavour, and season with salt and pepper. Add the wine and keep over a high heat for about 2 minutes until the wine evaporates.

③ Reduce the heat, cover and simmer gently for about 10 minutes until the leeks are soft.

PREPARATION AND COOKING TIME: 20 MINUTES

BRAISED CELERY HEARTS WITH ORANGE

—— SERVES 4 ——

✎ ⊕ ❄ I MONTH	METRIC	IMPERIAL	AMERICAN
Onion, quartered	I	I	I
Butter or margarine	25 g	I oz	2 tbsp
Carrot, quartered	I	I	I
Celery sticks	2	2	2
Chicken or vegetable stock	300 ml	½ pt	1¼ cups
Grated rind and juice of I orange			
Salt and freshly ground black pepper			

① Fit the metal blade. Process the onion for 4–5 seconds until chopped.

② Melt the butter or margarine and fry (sauté) the onion for a few minutes until softened but not browned.

③ Fit the slicing disc and slice the carrots and celery. Add to the onion, then pour over the stock. Add the orange rind and juice, and season well. Pour into a casserole dish (Dutch oven), cover and cook in a preheated oven at 160°C/325°F/gas mark 3 for 1–1½ hours until tender.

PREPARATION AND COOKING TIME: 2 HOURS

CARROTS WITH CARDAMOM

—— SERVES 4 ——

	METRIC	IMPERIAL	AMERICAN
Carrots	450 g	I lb	I lb
Butter or margarine	50 g	2 oz	¼ cup
Ground cardamom	2.5 ml	½ tsp	½ tsp

① Fit the slicing disc and slice the carrots.

② Place in a casserole dish (Dutch oven), dot with the butter or margarine and sprinkle with the cardamom. Cover and bake in a preheated oven at 180°C/350°F/gas mark 4 for 30–40 minutes, stirring once or twice during cooking.

PREPARATION AND COOKING TIME: 45 MINUTES

CELERIAC AU GRATIN

—— SERVES 4 ——

✳ ✦ ✎ ❄ 2 MONTHS	METRIC	IMPERIAL	AMERICAN
Cheddar cheese	50 g	2 oz	2 oz
Medium celeriac (celery root)	1	1	1
Slice of bread	1	1	1
Plain (all-purpose) flour	25 g	1 oz	¼ cup
Butter or margarine	25 g	1 oz	2 tbsp
Milk	450 ml	¾ pt	2 cups
Chopped parsley	15 ml	1 tbsp	1 tbsp
Salt and freshly ground black pepper			

① Fit the grating disc and grate the cheese, then remove from the bowl.

② Fit the slicing disc and slice the celeriac.

③ Boil the celeriac in salted water for 3–4 minutes, then drain well.

④ Fit the metal blade. With the motor running, drop pieces of the bread through the feed tube to make breadcrumbs. Remove from the bowl.

⑤ Process the flour, butter or margarine and milk for 10 seconds until well blended. Pour into a pan and bring to the boil, stirring continuously, then simmer gently for a further 1 minute, stirring. Remove from the heat and stir in half the cheese. Season to taste with salt and pepper.

⑥ Arrange the cooked celeriac slices in a casserole dish (Dutch oven) and pour over the sauce. Mix together the breadcrumbs and the remaining cheese and sprinkle over the top.

⑦ Bake in a preheated oven at 190°C/375°F/gas mark 5 for 15 minutes until golden brown.

PREPARATION AND COOKING TIME: 25 MINUTES

CARROT AND LENTIL PURÉE

—— SERVES 4 ——

⊕ ✎ ✳ 3 MONTHS	METRIC	IMPERIAL	AMERICAN
Medium potato	1	1	1
Carrots	225 g	8 oz	8 oz
Lentils	100 g	4 oz	⅔ cup
Butter or margarine, cut into pieces	25 g	1 oz	2 tbsp
Salt and freshly ground black pepper			
Single (light) cream	15 ml	1 tbsp	1 tbsp

① Fit the slicing disc and slice the potato and carrots.

② Cook in boiling salted water for about 5 minutes until just soft. Drain well.

③ Place the lentils in a pan with just enough water to cover, bring to the boil, then simmer gently for 20 minutes or until the lentils are soft and all the water has been absorbed. The cooking time will vary depending on the type, quality and freshness of the lentils.

④ Fit the metal blade and process the lentils for about 10 seconds until you have a smooth purée. Add the carrots, potatoes and butter or margarine and season well with salt and pepper. Process for about 8 seconds to a purée. Add the cream and mix for a few seconds until blended.

PREPARATION AND COOKING TIME: 30 MINUTES

POTATOES ANNA

—— SERVES 4 ——

⊕	METRIC	IMPERIAL	AMERICAN
Potatoes	450 g	1 lb	1 lb
Butter or margarine	25 g	1 oz	2 tbsp
Milk	120 ml	4 fl oz	½ cup
Salt and freshly ground black pepper			

① Fit the slicing disc and thinly slice the potatoes.

② Arrange in a casserole dish (Dutch oven) in overlapping layers. About halfway through, dot with half the butter or margarine, then finish with the rest of the potatoes and dot with the remaining butter or margarine.

③ Season the milk with salt and pepper and pour over the potatoes. Cover with foil.

④ Bake in a preheated oven at 190°C/375°F/gas mark 5 for about 1 hour until soft throughout and golden on top.

PREPARATION AND COOKING TIME: 1 HOUR 10 MINUTES

STIR-FRIED VEGETABLES

—— SERVES 4 ——

⊕ ⊗	METRIC	IMPERIAL	AMERICAN
Leeks	2	2	2
Small red (bell) pepper, halved	I	I	I
Small green pepper, halved	I	I	I
White cabbage	100 g	4 oz	4 oz
Large carrot	I	I large	I large
Oil	30 ml	2 tbsp	2 tbsp
Dry sherry	30 ml	2 tbsp	2 tbsp
Soy sauce	15 ml	I tbsp	I tbsp
Salt and freshly ground black pepper			

① Fit the slicing disc and slice first the leeks, then the peppers and cabbage, removing each one from the bowl when finished.

② Fit the grating disc and grate the carrot.

③ Heat the oil in a wok or large frying pan (skillet). Add the leeks and stir-fry for 2–3 minutes until hot and well coated in oil. Add the peppers and stir-fry for 2–3 minutes. Add the cabbage and stir-fry for 1 minute.

④ Mix together the sherry and soy sauce and season well with salt and pepper. Pour into the pan and toss well to incorporate the flavours. Serve immediately.

PREPARATION AND COOKING TIME: 10 MINUTES

RATATOUILLE

—— SERVES 4 ——

⊕ ⟲ ❄ 3 MONTHS	METRIC	IMPERIAL	AMERICAN
Aubergine (eggplant)	I	I	I
Onions, quartered	350 g	12 oz	12 oz
Courgettes (zucchini)	225 g	8 oz	8 oz
Green (bell) pepper, quartered	I	I	I
Red pepper, quartered	I	I	I
Garlic clove, halved	I	I	I
Olive oil	45 ml	3 tbsp	3 tbsp
Can of tomatoes	400 g	14 oz	I large
Chopped parsley	15 ml	I tbsp	I tbsp
Dried oregano	5 ml	I tsp	I tsp
Salt and freshly ground black pepper			

① Fit the slicing disc and slice the aubergine. Arrange on a flat plate, sprinkle with salt and leave to stand for 30 minutes.

② Slice the onions and remove from the bowl. Slice the courgettes and remove. Slice the peppers and remove.

③ Fit the metal blade. With the motor running, drop the garlic through the feed tube and process for a few seconds until chopped. Remove from the bowl.

④ Heat the oil in a large frying pan (skillet) and fry (sauté) the onion and garlic for about 4 minutes until just soft. Add the peppers and fry for 3–4 minutes until soft, then add the courgettes.

⑤ Rinse and drain the aubergine, then pat dry on kitchen paper (paper towels). Add to the pan with the tomatoes and herbs, and season to taste with salt and pepper. Stir well, then turn into a casserole dish (Dutch oven).

⑥ Cook in a preheated oven at 180°C/350°F/gas mark 4 for 1½ hours until soft.

⑦ Serve hot or cold as a side dish or with crusty bread as a starter.

PREPARATION AND COOKING TIME: 2 HOURS

SALADS

The versatility of your food processor really comes to the fore when preparing salads. Slicing, chopping, grating – it's all done in seconds, and you don't have to wash out the bowl between ingredients if you are making any kind of mixed salad.

And, of course, when all the salad stuffs are ready, your food processor can be used to make the dressing!

COLESLAW WITH GRAPES

—— SERVES 4 ——

⊕ ⊛ ⟡	METRIC	IMPERIAL	AMERICAN
White cabbage	450 g	1 lb	1 lb
Red eating (dessert) apple, quartered and cored	1	1	1
Carrots	3	3	3
Onion, quartered	1	1	1
Seedless grapes, halved	225 g	8 oz	8 oz
Olive oil	90 ml	6 tbsp	6 tbsp
White wine vinegar	30 ml	2 tbsp	2 tbsp
Caraway seeds	2.5 ml	½ tsp	½ tsp
Caster (superfine) sugar	2.5 ml	½ tsp	½ tsp
Salt and freshly ground black pepper			

① Fit the slicing disc. Cut the white cabbage to fit the feed tube, removing the hard stalk. Slice, then transfer to a large bowl. Slice the apple and add to the cabbage.

② Fit the grating disc. Grate the carrots and add to the cabbage. Grate the onion and add to the cabbage with the grapes.

③ Fit the metal blade. Place the oil, wine vinegar, caraway seeds and sugar in the processor and process for 3–4 seconds until the dressing thickens. Season to taste with salt and pepper.

④ Add the dressing to the prepared ingredients, tossing everything so that it is well incorporated. Serve immediately.

PREPARATION TIME: 10 MINUTES

SALADE NIÇOISE

—— SERVES 4 ——

⊕ ⊛	METRIC	IMPERIAL	AMERICAN
French (green) beans	225 g	8 oz	8 oz
Salt			
Tomatoes	225 g	8 oz	8 oz
Cooked potatoes	225 g	8 oz	8 oz
Cucumber	½	½	½
Can of tuna	200 g	7 oz	I small
Lemon juice	10 ml	2 tsp	2 tsp
Black olives, stoned (pitted)	8	8	8
Can of anchovies (optional)	50 g	2 oz	I small
Freshly ground black pepper			

① Bring a pan of salted water to the boil, add the French beans and cook for about 5 minutes until tender but still crisp. Drain and rinse under cold water, then cut into small pieces.

② Fit the slicing disc. Slice the tomatoes, use half to cover the base of a salad bowl and reserve the remainder. Slice the potatoes and about one-third of the cucumber and reserve.

③ Fit the grating disc. Peel and grate the remaining cucumber.

④ Place the beans, sliced potatoes, grated cucumber, the tuna and the oil from its can into a bowl and mix gently, breaking up the tuna slightly. Stir in the lemon juice, then spoon over the tomatoes in the salad bowl.

⑤ Arrange the cucumber slices on top of the tuna mixture, then arrange the remaining tomato slices in the centre. Garnish with the olives and anchovy fillets, if liked. Chill well before serving.

PREPARATION TIME: 15 MINUTES

RAW VEGETABLE SALAD

—— SERVES 4 ——

⊕ ⊗	METRIC	IMPERIAL	AMERICAN
White cabbage	¼	¼	¼
Celery sticks	2	2	2
Carrots	225 g	8 oz	8 oz
Celeriac (celery root)	½	½	½
Cooked beetroot (red beet)	225 g	8 oz	8 oz
Olive oil	90 ml	6 tbsp	6 tbsp
White wine vinegar	30 ml	2 tbsp	2 tbsp
Chopped tarragon	5 ml	1 tsp	1 tsp
French mustard	5 ml	1 tsp	1 tsp
Salt and freshly ground black pepper			

① Fit the slicing disc. Cut the cabbage to fit the feed tube. Slice the cabbage and place in a serving dish. Slice the celery and add to the cabbage.

② Fit the grating disc. Grate the carrots and celeriac and place in the dish. Grate the beetroot and place in a separate dish.

③ Wash the processor bowl and fit the metal blade. Process the oil, wine vinegar, tarragon, mustard, salt and pepper for 10–12 seconds until the dressing thickens.

④ Spoon a little of the dressing over the beetroot, then pour the remainder over the salad and toss together well. Chill both for about 1 hour.

⑤ Just before serving, toss the salad and again and serve sprinkled with the beetroot.

PREPARATION TIME: 10 MINUTES PLUS CHILLING

AVOCADO AND BACON SALAD

—— SERVES 4 ——

✑⊕	METRIC	IMPERIAL	AMERICAN
Rashers (slices) of streaky bacon, rinded	6	6	6
Avocados, peeled, stoned (pitted) and quartered	2	2	2
Lemon juice	15 ml	1 tbsp	1 tbsp
Olive oil	30 ml	2 tbsp	2 tbsp
Salt and freshly ground black pepper			

① Fit the metal blade and process the bacon until chopped.

② Fry (sauté) the bacon without extra fat until crisp.

③ Fit the slicing disc. Stand the avocado quarters two at a time in the feed tube and slice. Arrange in a shallow bowl.

④ Fit the metal blade. Scrape down any pieces of avocado and add the lemon juice, oil and salt and pepper. Process for 5 seconds until thick. Pour over the avocado slices.

⑤ Sprinkle with the bacon and chill before serving.

PREPARATION AND COOKING TIME: 15 MINUTES PLUS CHILLING

CUCUMBER RAITA

—— SERVES 4 ——

	METRIC	IMPERIAL	AMERICAN
Cucumber, peeled	½	½	½
Plain yoghurt	150 ml	5 fl oz	⅔ cup
Snipped chives	30 ml	2 tbsp	2 tbsp

① Fit the grating disc and grate the cucumber. Mix with the yoghurt, then sprinkle with the snipped chives.

② Serve as a side dish with curry.

PREPARATION TIME: 10 MINUTES

LEMON FENNEL SALAD
—— SERVES 4 ——

⊕ ☜	METRIC	IMPERIAL	AMERICAN
Head of fennel	I	I	I
Lemon	I	I	I
Olive oil	30 ml	2 tbsp	2 tbsp
Plain yoghurt	30 ml	2 tbsp	2 tbsp
Caster (superfine) sugar	10 ml	2 tsp	2 tsp
Salt and freshly ground black pepper			
Black olives, stoned (pitted)	6	6	6

① Fit the slicing disc. Trim the fennel to fit the feed tube, then slice and remove from the bowl.

② Fit the metal blade. Trim the peel and pith off half the lemon, then cut into thick slices. Process the lemon slices for 5–6 seconds until finely chopped.

③ Squeeze 15 ml/1 tbsp juice from the other half of the lemon, add to the processor with the oil, yoghurt and sugar, and season to taste with salt and pepper. Process for 6–7 seconds until thick.

④ Toss the fennel in the dressing, then arrange on a serving plate and garnish with the olives.

PREPARATION TIME: 10 MINUTES

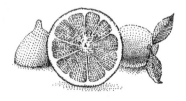

WALDORF SALAD

—— SERVES 4 ——

	METRIC	IMPERIAL	AMERICAN
Walnuts	50 g	2 oz	½ cup
Head of Chinese leaves (stem lettuce)	½	½	½
Red eating (dessert) apples, quartered and cored	2	2	2
Lemon juice	30 ml	2 tbsp	2 tbsp
Olive oil	90 ml	6 tbsp	6 tbsp
White wine vinegar	45 ml	3 tbsp	3 tbsp
Caster (superfine) sugar	5 ml	I tsp	I tsp
Salt and freshly ground black pepper			

① Fit the metal blade. Process the walnuts for 3–4 seconds until roughly chopped, then transfer to a serving bowl.

② Fit the slicing disc and slice the Chinese leaves, then add to the serving bowl. Slice the apples, then remove from the bowl and sprinkle with the lemon juice. Add to the serving bowl.

③ Place the oil, vinegar, sugar, salt and pepper in the processor and process for 10 seconds until thick and well blended. Just before serving, pour over the salad and toss the ingredients together well.

PREPARATION TIME: 10 MINUTES

A quick and simple sauce can transform the simplest of meals, so use your processor to make accompaniments to grilled (broiled) meats, chicken or fish to liven up your everyday meals.

Dessert sauces are simple too. For a quick fruit sauce, process about 225 g/8 oz of soft fruit until puréed – blackcurrants or raspberries work particularly well – then make up to 450 ml/¾ pt/2 cups with water, stir in 10 ml/ 2 tsp of cornflour (cornstarch) and bring to the boil, stirring continuously until the sauce thickens.

Apple sauce can easily be made by puréeing apples stewed with a little sugar and lemon juice; serve hot or cold.

For extra speed, save oddments of cheese that are usually thrown away and grate them in the processor. Freeze in a plastic bag or tub, to be added to sauces or toppings when required, straight from the freezer.

WHITE SAUCE

—— SERVES 4 ——

	METRIC	IMPERIAL	AMERICAN
Milk	450 ml	¾ pt	2 cups
Plain (all-purpose) flour	25 g	1 oz	¼ cup
Butter or margarine	25 g	1 oz	2 tbsp
Salt and freshly ground black pepper			

① Fit the metal blade. Place the milk, flour and butter or margarine in the processor and process until the fat is finely chopped and all the ingredients are well mixed.

② Pour the mixture into a saucepan and bring to the boil, then simmer very gently, stirring continuously, for about 5 minutes until the sauce thickens enough to coat the back of a spoon.

③ Season to taste with salt and pepper.

Tip: For extra flavour, before making the sauce, bring the milk to the boil with an onion and a bay leaf, then cover and leave to infuse for 30 minutes. Strain before continuing with the recipe.

PREPARATION AND COOKING TIME: 10 MINUTES

Cheese Sauce: Grate 100 g/4 oz of Cheddar or other hard cheese, then remove it from the bowl and make the sauce as above. Add the grated cheese with the seasoning and stir until melted.

Mustard Sauce: Whisk 15 ml/1 tbsp of French mustard, 5 ml/1 tsp of sugar, 5 ml/1 tsp of white wine vinegar and a knob of butter into the finished sauce.

Parsley Sauce: Remove the stalks from a bunch of fresh parsley, place the leaves in the processor and chop finely, then remove from the bowl. Make the sauce as above, then stir in the finely chopped parsley with the seasoning.

MUSHROOM SAUCE

—— SERVES 4 ——

🗂 ❄ 4 MONTHS	METRIC	IMPERIAL	AMERICAN
Mushrooms	100 g	4 oz	4 oz
Oil	15 ml	I tbsp	I tbsp
Butter or margarine	25 g	I oz	2 tbsp
Plain (all-purpose) flour	25 g	I oz	¼ cup
Chicken or vegetable stock	300 ml	½ pt	I¼ cups
Tomato purée (paste)	15 ml	I tbsp	I tbsp
Salt and freshly ground black pepper			

① Fit the metal blade and process the mushrooms until finely chopped.

② Heat the oil and fry (sauté) the mushrooms for a few minutes until soft.

③ Process the butter or margarine, flour, stock and tomato purée for 10 seconds until well blended. Pour over the mushrooms, bring to the boil, stirring continuously, then simmer for 15 minutes until thickened.

PREPARATION AND COOKING TIME: 25 MINUTES

TOMATO AND LENTIL SAUCE

—— SERVES 4 ——

⊕ ✎ ❄ 3 MONTHS	METRIC	IMPERIAL	AMERICAN
Lentils	100 g	4 oz	⅔ cup
Onion, quartered	I	I	I
Green (bell) pepper	½	½	½
Olive oil	15 ml	I tbsp	I tbsp
Can of tomatoes	400 g	14 oz	I large
Dried mixed herbs	5 ml	I tsp	I tsp
Chopped basil leaves	15 ml	I tbsp	I tbsp
Salt and freshly ground black pepper			

① Cook the lentils in boiling water for about 20 minutes, according to the packet instructions. The cooking time will vary depending on the type, quality and freshness of the lentils.

② Meanwhile fit the slicing disc and slice the onion and pepper.

③ Heat the oil in a small saucepan and fry (sauté) the onion and pepper for about 5 minutes until soft.

④ Add the tomatoes and their juice and simmer for about 10–15 minutes. Add the lentils and herbs and season well with salt and pepper.

⑤ Fit the metal blade. Return the sauce to the processor and process for 10–15 seconds until smooth.

⑥ Use as an accompaniment for meat dishes or simply pour over freshly boiled pasta for a quick supper.

PREPARATION AND COOKING TIME: 20 MINUTES

Tomato Sauce: Omit the lentils to make a Tomato Sauce. Drain the can of tomatoes for a thicker sauce.

GARLIC MAYONNAISE
—— SERVES 4 ——

	METRIC	IMPERIAL	AMERICAN
Garlic clove, halved	1	1	1
Egg yolks	3	3	3
Salt	2.5 ml	½ tsp	½ tsp
English mustard powder	2.5 ml	½ tsp	½ tsp
White wine vinegar	30 ml	2 tbsp	2 tbsp
Olive or safflower oil	300 ml	½ pt	1¼ cups
Lemon juice	5 ml	1 tsp	1 tsp

① Fit the metal blade. With the motor running, drop the garlic through the feed tube and process for a few seconds until finely chopped.

② Add the egg yolks, salt, mustard and about one-third of the wine vinegar and process for 3–4 seconds until well combined.

③ With the motor running, add the oil through the feed tube in a thin, steady stream, holding the jug about 5 cm/2 in above the top of the feed tube. Process for a few seconds until the mixture thickens.

④ Add the remaining vinegar and lemon juice to taste and blend briefly to achieve a thick and glossy consistency.

Variation: If you are not a garlic lover, just omit the garlic to make plain mayonnaise.

PREPARATION TIME: 10 MINUTES

GREEN MAYONNAISE

—— SERVES 4 ——

	METRIC	IMPERIAL	AMERICAN
A bunch of watercress			
A bunch of parsley			
Garlic clove, halved	I	I	I
Salt	2.5 ml	½ tsp	½ tsp
Egg yolks	3	3	3
English mustard powder	2.5 ml	½ tsp	½ tsp
White wine vinegar	30 ml	2 tbsp	2 tbsp
Olive oil	300 ml	½ pt	I¼ cups
Lemon juice	5 ml	I tsp	I tsp

① Fit the metal blade. Remove any hard stalks from the watercress and parsley and process for 10–15 seconds until finely chopped. Remove from the bowl.

② With the motor running, drop the garlic through the feed tube and process until finely chopped. Add the salt, egg yolks, mustard and 5 ml/1 tsp of the wine vinegar and process for 3–4 seconds.

③ With the motor still running, add the oil through the feed tube in a very thin stream until the mayonnaise thickens and all the oil has been incorporated. Add the remaining wine vinegar and the lemon juice and process for 3–4 seconds.

④ Add the watercress and parsley and process for 3–4 seconds to mix.

⑤ Like all mayonnaise, this keeps well for a few days if stored in a screw-topped jar in the refrigerator.

PREPARATION TIME: 15 MINUTES

TARTARE SAUCE
—— SERVES 4 ——

	METRIC	IMPERIAL	AMERICAN
A few sprigs of parsley			
Egg yolks	2	2	2
Mustard powder	2.5 ml	½ tsp	½ tsp
White wine vinegar	5 ml	I tsp	I tsp
Olive oil	150 ml	¼ pt	⅔ cup
Hard-boiled (hard-cooked) egg, quartered	I	I	I
Capers	15 ml	I tbsp	I tbsp
Gherkins	3	3	3
Salt and freshly ground black pepper			

① Fit the metal blade. Process the parsley for a few seconds until chopped, then remove from the bowl.

② Process the egg yolks, mustard and wine vinegar for about 4 seconds until mixed. With the motor running, gradually add the oil through the feed tube until the mixture is thick.

③ Add the egg, capers, gherkins and parsley and blend for a few seconds until finely chopped and mixed.

PREPARATION TIME: 10 MINUTES

BREAD SAUCE

—— SERVES 4 ——

	METRIC	IMPERIAL	AMERICAN
Milk	300 ml	½ pt	1¼ cups
Onion, quartered	I	I	I
Bay leaf	I	I	I
Cloves	2	2	2
Slices of white bread	2	2	2
Butter or margarine	15 g	½ oz	I tbsp
Freshly ground black pepper			

① Pour the milk into a pan and add the onion, bay leaf and cloves. Bring to the boil, then remove from the heat and leave to infuse for 30 minutes.

② Fit the metal blade. With the motor running, drop pieces of the bread through the feed tube to make breadcrumbs.

③ Strain the milk into a clean pan and bring back to the boil. Stir in the breadcrumbs, then beat in the butter or margarine and season well with pepper. Stir over a low heat for about 10 minutes until smooth and thick.

PREPARATION AND COOKING TIME: 15 MINUTES PLUS INFUSING

WALNUT VINAIGRETTE
—— SERVES 4 ——

🐑	METRIC	IMPERIAL	AMERICAN
Walnut halves	6	6	6
Garlic clove, halved	1	1	1
White wine vinegar	15 ml	1 tbsp	1 tbsp
French mustard	2.5 ml	½ tsp	½ tsp
Olive oil	45 ml	3 tbsp	3 tbsp
Salt and freshly ground black pepper			

① Fit the metal blade. With the motor running, drop the walnut halves through the feed tube and process for 7 seconds until finely chopped.

② Add all the other ingredients, scrape down the sides and process for 10 seconds until the sauce thickens.

③ This will keep for up to a week if stored in the fridge in a screw-topped jar.

PREPARATION TIME: 5 MINUTES

MINT SAUCE
—— SERVES 4 ——

🐑	METRIC	IMPERIAL	AMERICAN
A bunch of mint			
Boiling water	15 ml	1 tbsp	1 tbsp
Caster (superfine) sugar	15 ml	1 tbsp	1 tbsp
White wine vinegar	30 ml	2 tbsp	2 tbsp
Orange juice	60 ml	4 tbsp	4 tbsp

① Fit the metal blade. Process the mint for 5–6 seconds until finely chopped. Add the boiling water and sugar and process for a few seconds to blend.

② Add the wine vinegar and orange juice and process again for a few seconds to mix.

PREPARATION TIME: 5 MINUTES

BUTTERSCOTCH SAUCE
—— SERVES 4 ——

	METRIC	IMPERIAL	AMERICAN
Butter, cut into pieces	25 g	1 oz	2 tbsp
Golden (light corn) syrup, warmed	30 ml	2 tbsp	2 tbsp
Demerara sugar	30 ml	2 tbsp	2 tbsp
Water	60 ml	4 tbsp	4 tbsp
Lemon juice	5 ml	1 tsp	1 tsp
Custard powder	10 ml	2 tsp	2 tsp

(1) Fit the metal blade. Process all the ingredients for 8–9 seconds until smooth.

(2) Pour the sauce into a small saucepan and heat gently, stirring continuously, until the sauce thickens.

(3) This rich, velvety sauce is delicious served hot over puddings or ice cream.

PREPARATION AND COOKING TIME: 10 MINUTES

FLUFFY ALMOND SAUCE
—— SERVES 4 ——

3 MONTHS	METRIC	IMPERIAL	AMERICAN
Blanched almonds	25 g	1 oz	¼ cup
Milk	600 ml	1 pt	2½ cups
Plain (all-purpose) flour	15 ml	1 tbsp	1 tbsp
Caster (superfine) sugar	15 ml	1 tbsp	1 tbsp
Egg, separated	1	1	1

(1) Fit the metal blade. Process the nuts for about 12 seconds until finely chopped. Add the milk, flour, sugar and egg yolk and process for a few seconds until smooth.

(2) Pour the mixture into a pan and bring to the boil, stirring continuously until thick. Leave to cool slightly, then process again for 10 seconds until smooth and thick.

(3) Whisk the egg white until stiff, then fold in.

(4) Serve warm with fruit puddings.

PREPARATION AND COOKING TIME: 10 MINUTES

DESSERTS

Perfect for mixing and grinding, for making purées or pastry (paste), using your food processor can really broaden your repertoire of simple, everyday desserts for the family, or make special-occasion desserts that much easier to achieve.

Make an easy fruit fool by poaching your favourite sharp fruit – such as rhubarb or gooseberries – then puréeing it in the processor and blending with some whipped cream or crème fraîche.

Don't forget that pancake batter is easily made in the processor (see page 51) and pancakes can be served sprinkled with lemon juice and sugar or stuffed with sweet fillings. However, egg whites for meringues and cream for piping are not successful in all machines – check your instruction booklet or experiment with your machine.

APPLE AND WALNUT FLAN

—— SERVES 4 ——

🐾 ⊕ ❄ 6 MONTHS	METRIC	IMPERIAL	AMERICAN
Butter or margarine, cut into pieces	100 g	4 oz	½ cup
Plain (all-purpose) flour	175 g	6 oz	1½ cups
Caster (superfine) sugar	50 g	2 oz	¼ cup
Egg yolk	1	1	1
Cold water	15 ml	1 tbsp	1 tbsp
For the filling:			
Cooking (tart) apples, peeled, cored and quartered	450 g	1 lb	1 lb
Walnuts	25 g	1 oz	¼ cup
Whipping cream	150 ml	¼ pt	⅔ cup
Eggs	2	2	2
Caster (superfine) sugar	50 g	2 oz	¼ cup
Ground cinnamon	2.5 ml	½ tsp	½ tsp
Cream or ice cream, to serve			

① Fit the metal blade and process the butter or margarine, flour and sugar for 10 seconds until the mixture resembles fine breadcrumbs. Mix the egg yolk and water. With the motor running, pour the mixture through the feed tube and process for 6–7 seconds until the mixture just begins to hold together.

② Turn out on to a lightly floured board and pull together into a ball. Roll out and use to line a 23 cm/9 in flan ring. Chill in the fridge while preparing the filling.

③ Fit the slicing disc and slice the apples, then arrange them in the flan case (pie shell).

④ Fit the metal blade. Process the walnuts for 5 seconds until chopped. Add the cream, eggs, sugar and cinnamon and process for 5 seconds. Pour over the apples.

⑤ Bake in a preheated oven at 200°C/400°F/gas mark 6 for 10 minutes, then reduce the oven temperature to 180°C/350°F/gas mark 4 for a further 30 minutes.

⑥ Serve warm with cream or ice cream.

PREPARATION AND COOKING TIME: 50 MINUTES

CRUNCHY-TOPPED APPLE PIE

—— SERVES 4–6 ——

⊕ ☜ ❋ 3 MONTHS	METRIC	IMPERIAL	AMERICAN
Cooking (tart) apples, peeled, cored and quartered	450 g	I lb	I lb
Orange juice	30 ml	2 tbsp	2 tbsp
Caster (superfine) sugar	15 ml	I tbsp	I tbsp
Plain (all-purpose) flour	175 g	6 oz	I½ cups
A pinch of salt			
Butter or margarine, cut into pieces	100 g	4 oz	½ cup
Water	45 ml	3 tbsp	3 tbsp
Almonds	25 g	I oz	¼ cup
Honey	15 ml	I tbsp	I tbsp
Hot water	15 ml	I tbsp	I tbsp

① Fit the slicing disc and slice the apples. Arrange in a pie dish and sprinkle with the orange juice and caster sugar.

② Fit the metal blade. Process the flour, salt and butter or margarine for 8–10 seconds until the mixture resembles fine breadcrumbs. With the motor running, gradually add the cold water through the feed tube until the mixture forms a ball around the blade. Turn out on to a lightly floured surface and pull into a ball, then roll out to cover the pie dish, sealing the edges to the dish.

③ Process the almonds for 3–4 seconds until chopped. Stir the honey into the hot water, add to the almonds and process for 3 seconds until well mixed, then brush evenly over the pastry (paste).

④ Bake in a preheated oven at 190°C/375°F/gas mark 5 for 30–35 minutes until the top is crisp and golden.

Freezing tip: Freeze before baking. When required, thaw at room temperature for 3–4 hours, then bake as above.

PREPARATION AND COOKING TIME: 45 MINUTES

RICH CHOCOLATE PUDDING
—— SERVES 4 ——

🌿	METRIC	IMPERIAL	AMERICAN
Soft brown sugar	100 g	4 oz	½ cup
Self-raising (self-rising) flour	100 g	4 oz	1 cup
Baking powder	5 ml	1 tsp	1 tsp
Cocoa (unsweetened chocolate) powder	30 ml	2 tbsp	2 tbsp
Butter or margarine, cut into pieces	100 g	4 oz	½ cup
Eggs	2	2	2
For the sauce:			
Cocoa powder	15 ml	1 tbsp	1 tbsp
Cornflour (cornstarch)	5 ml	1 tsp	1 tsp
Caster (superfine) sugar	10 ml	2 tsp	2 tsp
Water	150 ml	¼ pt	⅔ cup
Custard or cream, to serve			

① Fit the metal blade. Process the brown sugar, flour, baking powder and cocoa power for a few seconds until mixed. Add the butter or margarine and eggs and process for 8–10 seconds until smooth.

② Spoon the mixture into a generously buttered 900 ml/ 2 pt/5 cup pudding basin.

③ Process the sauce ingredients for 4–5 seconds until mixed. Pour over the pudding and leave to stand for 5 minutes.

④ Bake in a preheated oven at 190°C/375°F/gas mark 5 for 40–45 minutes. Loosen the sides of the pudding and turn out on to a serving dish. The pudding should be moist and soggy on top with a crisper base.

⑤ Serve with custard or cream.

PREPARATION AND COOKING TIME: 1 HOUR

WALNUT BAKEWELL WITH PEARS

—— SERVES 4 ——

🐄 ⊕ ❋ 3 MONTHS	METRIC	IMPERIAL	AMERICAN
Plain (all-purpose) flour	175 g	6 oz	1½ cups
Butter or margarine, cut into pieces	75 g	3 oz	⅓ cup
Water	45 ml	3 tbsp	3 tbsp
Pears, peeled, cored and quartered	2	2	2
Walnuts	50 g	2 oz	½ cup
Self-raising (self-rising) flour	100 g	4 oz	1 cup
Soft (tub) margarine	100 g	4 oz	½ cup
Soft brown sugar	100 g	4 oz	½ cup
Eggs	2	2	2
Baking powder	5 ml	1 tsp	1 tsp
Cream or custard, to serve			

① Fit the metal blade. Process the plain flour and butter or margarine until the mixture resembles fine breadcrumbs. With the motor running, add the water gradually through the feed tube until the mixture just forms a ball around the blade.

② Turn out on to a lightly floured surface, pull together into a ball with the fingertips, then roll out and use the pastry (paste) to line a greased 23 cm/9 in flan tin (pan). Reserve the trimmings.

③ Fit the slicing disc and slice the pears, then arrange in the flan case (pie shell).

④ Fit the metal blade. Process the walnuts for 10 seconds until finely chopped. Add the self-raising flour, soft margarine, sugar, eggs and baking powder and process for 8–10 seconds until well combined. Spread the mixture over the pears.

⑤ Re-roll the pastry trimmings, cut into long strips and make a lattice over the filling, moistening the ends to seal to the base.

⑥ Bake in a preheated oven at 180°C/350°F/gas mark 4 for 30–35 minutes until well risen and golden brown.

⑦ Serve warm with cream or custard.

PREPARATION AND COOKING TIME: 50 MINUTES

CREAMY BANANA PIE

—— SERVES 4 ——

✎ ✿	METRIC	IMPERIAL	AMERICAN
Hazelnuts (filberts)	25 g	I oz	¼ cup
Plain (all-purpose) flour	100 g	4 oz	I cup
Butter or margarine, cut into pieces	75 g	3 oz	⅓ cup
Caster (superfine) sugar	75 g	3 oz	⅓ cup
Water	30 ml	2 tbsp	2 tbsp
Custard powder	25 g	I oz	2 tbsp
Egg yolk	I	I	I
Milk	450 ml	¾ pt	2 cups
Whipping cream	30 ml	2 tbsp	2 tbsp
Large bananas	2	2	2
Plain (semi-sweet) chocolate	25 g	I oz	I oz

① Fit the metal blade. Process the hazelnuts for about 10–12 seconds until finely chopped. Add the flour, butter or margarine and 50 g/2 oz/½ cup of the caster sugar and process for 6–7 seconds until the mixture looks like breadcrumbs. Add the water through the feed tube and process for a few seconds until the mixture forms a ball.

② Turn out on to a lightly floured surface, pull into a ball with the fingertips, then roll out and use to line a greased 20 cm/8 in flan ring. Prick the base with a fork and bake in a preheated oven at 200°C/400°F/gas mark 6 for 20–25 minutes until just brown around the edges.

③ Process the custard powder, the remaining caster sugar, the egg yolk and 45 ml/3 tbsp of the milk for 7–8 seconds.

④ Bring the rest of the milk to the boil in a small pan. With the motor running, pour in through the feed tube and process for 4–5 seconds until smooth. Return to the pan and heat, stirring continuously, until the sauce thickens.

⑤ Return to the processor and process for 7–8 seconds. With the motor running, add the cream through the tube.

⑥ Slice the bananas and arrange in the flan case (pie shell). Pour the custard mixture over the top and leave to cool.

⑦ Fit the grating disc, grate the chocolate and sprinkle over.

PREPARATION AND COOKING TIME: 45 MINUTES

ORANGE SAVARIN

—— SERVES 4–6 ——

🐟 ⊕ ❋ 2 MONTHS	METRIC	IMPERIAL	AMERICAN
Strong plain (bread) flour	100 g	4 oz	1 cup
Sachet of fast-action dried yeast	1	1	1
A pinch of sugar			
Milk, lukewarm	90 ml	6 tbsp	6 tbsp
Eggs, lightly beaten	2	2	2
Butter or margarine, cut into pieces	75 g	3 oz	⅓ cup
Granulated sugar	100 g	4 oz	½ cup
Water	150 ml	¼ pt	⅔ cup
Large orange	1	1	1
Rum or brandy	15 ml	1 tbsp	1 tbsp
Double (heavy) or whipping cream, to serve			

① Fit the metal blade. Process the flour, yeast and sugar for a few seconds until mixed. With the motor running, pour in the milk through the feed tube, then pour in the eggs and drop in the pieces of butter or margarine one at a time, incorporating each one before adding the next. Process for 10 seconds.

② Pour the mixture into a lightly oiled 20 cm/8 in savarin mould, cover with clingfilm (plastic wrap) and leave to rise for 45 minutes. Remove the clingfilm and bake in a preheated oven at 230°C/450°F/gas mark 8 for 30 minutes.

③ Meanwhile, dissolve the granulated sugar in the water over a low heat. Use a potato peeler to remove three or four strips of orange rind and add these to the syrup. Bring to the boil, boil for 1 minutes, then add the rum or brandy and remove from the heat.

④ Turn the savarin out of the mould on to a serving plate. Pour over the syrup and leave to soak in.

⑤ Fit the slicing disc. Quarter the orange, fit one quarter upright in the feed tube and slice, then arrange around the savarin. Remove the flesh from the remaining segments, cut each piece in half and use to fill the centre.

⑥ Whip the cream until stiff and serve with the savarin.

PREPARATION AND COOKING TIME: 50 MINUTES PLUS RISING

PEAR AND HAZELNUT SHORTCAKE

—— SERVES 4 ——

🕐 ⊕ ❄ I MONTH	METRIC	IMPERIAL	AMERICAN
Hazelnuts (filberts)	75 g	3 oz	¾ cup
Butter or margarine, cut into pieces	100 g	4 oz	½ cup
Caster (superfine) sugar	50 g	2 oz	¼ cup
Plain (all-purpose) flour	150 g	5 oz	1¼ cups
Water	15 ml	I tbsp	I tbsp
Pears	2	2	2
Double (heavy) cream	150 ml	¼ pt	⅔ cup
Icing (confectioners') sugar, sifted	15 ml	I tbsp	I tbsp

① Fit the metal blade and process the hazelnuts for 10 seconds until ground. Remove from the bowl.

② Process the butter or margarine and sugar for 5 seconds until mixed. Add the nuts and flour and process for 5 seconds. Stop and scrape down the sides of the bowl, then mix again for 5 seconds. With the motor running, add the water through the feed tube and mix for about 5 seconds. The mixture will not quite form a ball around the blade.

③ Tip out on to a lightly floured work surface and press it together with your fingertips. Divide in half and form into two balls. Roll or pat each one to an 18 cm/7 in circle. Place on a greased baking (cookie) sheet.

④ Bake in a preheated oven at 190°C/375°F/gas mark 5 for 10–12 minutes until just beginning to brown. Cut one circle into eight segments. Allow to cool on the trays.

⑤ Just before serving, peel, core and quarter the pears and slice using the slicing disc. Whip the cream until stiff.

⑥ Place the circle of shortcake on a serving dish, spread over about half the cream, then arrange the pear slices on top. Spoon or pipe the remaining cream over the pears, then reassemble the shortbread segments so they are resting at an angle on top of the cake. Sprinkle with icing sugar and serve at once.

Tip: You can make this dish with drained, canned fruit.

PREPARATION AND COOKING TIME: 20 MINUTES

REAL FOOD FROM YOUR FOOD PROCESSOR

PROFITEROLES WITH CHOCOLATE SAUCE

—— SERVES 4 ——

🌼 4 MONTHS	METRIC	IMPERIAL	AMERICAN
Butter	75 g	3 oz	⅓ cup
Water	500 ml	17 fl oz	2¼ cups
Plain (all-purpose) flour	100 g	4 oz	1 cup
Eggs	3	3	3
Whipping cream	150 ml	¼ pt	⅔ cup
Plain (semi-sweet) chocolate	175 g	6 oz	6 oz
Granulated sugar	100 g	4 oz	½ cup

① Place the butter in a small pan with 200 ml/7 fl oz/scant 1 cup of the water and bring to the boil, lifting it off the heat just as it begins to rise up in the pan.

② Fit the metal blade and place the flour in the processor. With the motor running, pour in the butter and water mixture through the feed tube and process for 10 seconds until smooth. Add the eggs one at a time and process for a further 10 seconds until the mixture is smooth and glossy.

③ Pipe or place spoonfuls of the mixture on a lightly greased baking (cookie) sheet and bake in a preheated oven at 220°C/425°F/gas mark 7 for 12–15 minutes until well risen and golden.

④ Remove from the oven and pierce the side of each profiterole to allow steam to escape. Allow to cool.

⑤ Whip the cream and pipe into the profiteroles.

⑥ Process the chocolate for 10–12 seconds until chopped. Place in a pan with the sugar and remaining water and heat gently, stirring, until the chocolate has melted. Bring to the boil, then simmer for 10–15 minutes.

⑦ Pile the profiteroles into a serving dish or individual dishes and pour over the sauce.

Freezing tip: Only the choux buns can be frozen. Open-freeze until hard, then pack in freezer bags. When required, thaw at room temperature for 3–4 hours.

PREPARATION AND COOKING TIME: 25 MINUTES

APRICOT CHEESECAKE

—— SERVES 6 ——

🌼 2 MONTHS	METRIC	IMPERIAL	AMERICAN
Digestive biscuits (Graham crackers)	12	12	12
Butter, cut into pieces	75 g	3 oz	⅓ cup
Can of apricots	425 g	15 oz	1 large
Sachet of gelatine	1	1	1
Cream cheese	100 g	4 oz	½ cup
Double (heavy) or whipping cream	150 ml	¼ pt	⅔ cup
Flaked (slivered) almonds	30 ml	2 tbsp	2 tbsp

① Fit the metal blade. Roughly break up the biscuits as you put them in the processor. Add the butter and process for 15 seconds until well combined. Press into the base of an 20 cm/8 in flan ring. Chill.

② Drain the apricots, reserve two for decoration and place 90 ml/6 tbsp of the juice from the can in a small bowl. Sprinkle over the gelatine and leave for a few minutes until spongy, then place the bowl in a pan of warm water for a few minutes until dissolved.

③ Process the cream cheese for 15 seconds until soft. Add the drained apricots and process for 10 seconds until blended. Scrape down the sides of the bowl, add the cream and process for 10 seconds.

④ With the motor running, pour the gelatine mixture in through the feed tube and process for 5 seconds. Pour over the biscuit base and chill for 1 hour.

⑤ Decorate with the reserved apricots and the flaked almonds.

PREPARATION TIME: 20 MINUTES PLUS CHILLING

CHOCOLATE CHIP ICE CREAM

—— SERVES 4 ——

🥄 ❄ 2 MONTHS	METRIC	IMPERIAL	AMERICAN
Plain (semi-sweet) chocolate	50 g	2 oz	2 oz
Eggs	2	2	2
Egg yolks	2	2	2
Caster (superfine) sugar	100 g	4 oz	½ cup
Milk	600 ml	1 pt	2½ cups
Double (heavy) cream	90 ml	6 tbsp	6 tbsp

① Fit the metal blade. Process the chocolate for
    10–12 seconds until chopped. Remove from the bowl.

② Process the eggs, egg yolks and sugar for 10 seconds.

③ Heat the milk in a pan. With the motor running, pour the
    milk through the feed tube and process for a few seconds
    until mixed. Pour the mixture back into the pan and heat,
    stirring continuously, until the mixture coats the back of
    a spoon. Pour into a freezer tray, cover with a piece of
    greaseproof (waxed) paper and leave to cool.

④ Place the chocolate mixture in the freezer for 2 hours
    until set around the edges and just icy in the middle.
    Place in the processor and process for 8–10 seconds until
    smooth. Add the cream and process for 8–10 seconds.
    Add the chocolate pieces and process for 2 seconds just to
    mix. Return to the freezer tray and freeze for 4–5 hours.

⑤ Remove from the freezer 20 minutes before serving to
    allow the ice cream to soften.

Tip: You can vary the flavour of the ice cream by using
fruit purée or chopped nuts instead of the chocolate.

PREPARATION TIME: 10 MINUTES PLUS FREEZING

PINEAPPLE SORBET

—— SERVES 4 ——

🍃 ❄ 2 MONTHS	METRIC	IMPERIAL	AMERICAN
Can of pineapple	400 g	14 oz	1 large
Water			
Granulated sugar	175 g	6 oz	¾ cup
Lemon	1	1	1
Egg white	1	1	1
A few sprigs of mint, to garnish			

① Drain the juice from the can of pineapple into a measuring jug and make up to 600 ml/1 pt/2½ cups with water, then add the sugar. Pour into a saucepan and heat gently until the sugar dissolves.

② Peel the lemon rind with a potato peeler, then add the strips to the sugar syrup and boil for 5 minutes. Squeeze the lemon and add the juice to the pan.

③ Fit the metal blade. Process the pineapple for 7–8 seconds until puréed. Add to the sugar syrup. Leave to cool.

④ Pour into a freezer tray and freeze for 2 hours until firm around the edges and slushy in the centre. Pour into the processor and process for about 7–8 seconds until smooth.

⑤ Whisk the egg white and add to the sorbet. Process for 2–3 seconds until mixed. Return to the freezer tray and freeze until firm. Serve straight from the freezer, garnished with sprigs of mint.

Tip: For special occasions, use a whole pineapple. Cut in half and scoop out the flesh. Pile the finished sorbet into the pineapple shell and decorate with fresh pineapple pieces.

PREPARATION TIME: 15 MINUTES PLUS FREEZING

ORANGE AND BANANA CREAMS
—— SERVES 4 ——

	METRIC	IMPERIAL	AMERICAN
Orange, peeled and quartered	I	I	I
Large ripe bananas, cut into chunks	3	3	3
Double (heavy) cream	150 ml	¼ pt	⅔ cup

① Fit the metal blade and process the orange flesh for 7–8 seconds until finely chopped. Add the bananas and process for 5–6 seconds until well mixed.

② With the motor running, pour in the cream through the feed tube and process for 5–6 seconds until thick.

③ Pour into individual dishes and chill before serving.

PREPARATION TIME: 5 MINUTES PLUS CHILLING

CAKES AND BISCUITS

All kinds of cake and biscuit (cookie) mixtures can be prepared in your food processor. When making fruit cakes, add the dried fruit or glacé (candied) cherries at the end and process for just a few seconds to avoid them being cut into tiny pieces.

Royal icing (frosting) that is glossy and easy to pipe can be made by mixing the egg white in the processor with the metal blade, and then adding the icing (confectioners') sugar gradually, in batches.

VICTORIA SANDWICH
—— SERVES 4–6 ——

	METRIC	IMPERIAL	AMERICAN
Self-raising (self-rising) flour	175 g	6 oz	1½ cups
Soft (tub) margarine, cut into pieces	175 g	6 oz	¾ cup
Caster (superfine) sugar	175 g	6 oz	¾ cup
Eggs	3	3	3
Baking powder	5 ml	1 tsp	1 tsp
Raspberry jam (conserve)	60 ml	4 tbsp	4 tbsp
Double (heavy) cream	150 ml	¼ pt	⅔ cup
Icing (confectioners') sugar	15 ml	1 tbsp	1 tbsp

① Fit the metal blade. Place the flour, margarine, sugar, eggs and baking powder in the food processor and process for 10–15 seconds until well blended.

② Turn out into two greased and lined 18 cm/7 in baking tins (pans).

③ Bake in a preheated oven at 180°C/350°F/gas mark 4 for 25–30 minutes until well risen and golden. The centres should spring back when pressed lightly with a fingertip. Remove from the tins and leave to cool.

④ Spread the jam over one of the cakes. Whip the cream until stiff, then spread it over the jam and top with the second cake. Sift the icing sugar over the top of the cake.

PREPARATION AND COOKING TIME: 40 MINUTES

ORANGE AND LEMON CAKE

—— SERVES 4–6 ——

✂ ❄ 4 MONTHS	METRIC	IMPERIAL	AMERICAN
Soft (tub) margarine, cut into pieces	100 g	4 oz	½ cup
Self-raising (self-rising) flour	100 g	4 oz	1 cup
Caster (superfine) sugar	100 g	4 oz	½ cup
Eggs	2	2	2
Juice and freshly grated rind of 1 orange			
Juice and freshly grated rind of 1 lemon			
Granulated sugar	30 ml	2 tbsp	2 tbsp

① Fit the metal blade. Process the margarine, flour, caster sugar and eggs for 10 seconds until smooth.

② Add the orange rind and 15 ml/1 tbsp of the orange juice to the cake mixture and process for 3–4 seconds to mix. Turn the mixture into a lightly greased 20 cm/8 in cake tin (pan).

③ Mix the lemon rind and juice with 15 ml/1 tbsp of the granulated sugar and spoon over the top of the cake.

④ Bake in a preheated oven at 180°C/350°F/gas mark 4 for 35–40 minutes until well risen and golden brown. Sprinkle with the remaining granulated sugar while still hot and allow to cool in the tin.

PREPARATION AND COOKING TIME: 50 MINUTES

DATE BREAD
—— SERVES 4–6 ——

🌼 3 MONTHS	METRIC	IMPERIAL	AMERICAN
Stoned (pitted) dates	75 g	3 oz	½ cup
Plain (all-purpose) flour	225 g	8 oz	2 cups
Soft brown sugar	150 g	5 oz	⅔ cup
Soft (tub) margarine, cut into pieces	50 g	2 oz	¼ cup
A pinch of salt			
Bicarbonate of soda (baking soda)	5 ml	1 tsp	1 tsp
Egg	1	1	1
Milk	100 ml	3½ fl oz	scant ½ cup

① Fit the metal blade. Process the dates for 5–6 seconds until evenly chopped. Remove from the bowl.

② Process the flour, sugar, margarine, salt and bicarbonate of soda for 10 seconds until blended. Add the dates, egg and milk and process for 7–8 seconds until all the ingredients are combined.

③ Place in a greased 900 g/2 lb loaf tin (pan) and bake at 180°C/350°F/gas mark 4 for 55–60 minutes until firm and golden. Leave to cool slightly in the tin, then turn out to finish cooling.

④ Serve thinly sliced and buttered.

PREPARATION AND COOKING TIME: 1 HOUR

WALNUT CAKE
—— SERVES 4–6 ——

🌼 6 MONTHS	METRIC	IMPERIAL	AMERICAN
Walnuts	75 g	3 oz	¾ cup
Soft (tub) margarine, cut into pieces	225 g	8 oz	1 cup
Self-raising (self-rising) flour	175 g	6 oz	1½ cups
Caster (superfine) sugar	175 g	6 oz	¾ cup
Baking powder	5 ml	1 tsp	1 tsp
Eggs	3	3	3

① Fit the metal blade. Process the nuts for 15–20 seconds
    until finely ground. Add the margarine, flour, sugar,
    baking powder and eggs and process for 12–15 seconds
    until well mixed. Turn into a lightly greased 20 cm/8 in
    cake tin (pan).

③ Bake in a preheated oven at 180°C/350°F/gas mark 4 for
    55 minutes until firm and golden. Allow to cool slightly
    in the tin before turning out.

    Variation: For a change, substitute hazelnuts (filberts) or
    almonds for the walnuts.

PREPARATION AND COOKING TIME: 1 HOUR

QUICK FRUIT CAKE

—— SERVES 4–6 ——

✿ 4 MONTHS	METRIC	IMPERIAL	AMERICAN
Self-raising (self-rising) flour	225 g	8 oz	2 cups
Baking powder	5 ml	1 tsp	1 tsp
Mixed (apple-pie) spice	5 ml	1 tsp	1 tsp
Caster (superfine) sugar	100 g	4 oz	½ cup
Soft (tub) margarine, cut into pieces	100 g	4 oz	½ cup
Eggs	2	2	2
Milk	75 ml	5 tbsp	5 tbsp
Dried mixed fruit (fruit cake mix)	50 g	2 oz	⅓ cup
Glacé (candied) cherries	50 g	2 oz	¼ cup
Demerara sugar	15 ml	1 tbsp	1 tbsp

① Fit the metal blade. Process the flour, baking powder,
    spice, sugar and margarine for 10 seconds until blended.
    Add the eggs, milk, fruit and glacé cherries and process
    for 7–8 seconds until the ingredients are just combined.

② Spoon into a greased and lined 20 cm/8 in cake tin (pan)
    and sprinkle the top with demerara sugar.

③ Bake in a preheated oven at 180°C/350°F/gas mark 4 for
    50–60 minutes until firm and a skewer inserted into the
    centre comes out clean. Leave to cool slightly in the tin
    before turning out.

PREPARATION AND COOKING TIME: 1 HOUR

DEVON SCONES
—— MAKES 8–10 ——

🖎	METRIC	IMPERIAL	AMERICAN
Self-raising (self-rising) flour	225 g	8 oz	2 cups
A pinch of salt			
Butter or margarine, cut into pieces	50 g	2 oz	¼ cup
Caster (superfine) sugar	25 g	1 oz	2 tbsp
Egg	1	1	1
Milk	120 ml	4 fl oz	½ cup
Butter, jam (conserve) and clotted cream, to serve			

① Fit the metal blade. Process the flour, salt, butter or margarine and sugar until the mixture resembles fine breadcrumbs.

② Break the egg into a measuring jug and make up to 150 ml/¼ pt/⅔ cup with the milk. Beat lightly.

③ With the motor running, pour the egg and milk mixture through the feed tube and process for a few seconds until the mixture binds together.

④ Tip out on to a lightly floured surface and pull together with the fingertips, then roll out to about 1 cm/½ in thick and cut into rounds with a 5 cm/2 in pastry (cookie) cutter. Arrange on a greased baking (cookie) sheet. Brush with any remaining milk.

⑤ Bake in a preheated oven at 220°C/425°F/gas mark 7 for 10 minutes until risen and golden brown. Leave to cool.

⑥ Serve split and buttered, with jam and clotted cream.

Variation: Add 25 g/1 oz/2 tbsp of glacé (candied) cherries and 5 ml/1 tsp of ground ginger to the dry ingredients to make Cherry and Ginger Scones.

PREPARATION AND COOKING TIME: 20 MINUTES

WHOLEMEAL CHEESE SCONES

—— MAKES ABOUT 12 ——

⊛ ✑	METRIC	IMPERIAL	AMERICAN
Cheddar cheese	75 g	3 oz	3 oz
Parmesan cheese	25 g	1 oz	1 oz
Plain (all-purpose) flour	100 g	4 oz	1 cup
Wholemeal flour	100 g	4 oz	1 cup
Mustard powder	2.5 ml	½ tsp	½ tsp
Baking powder	5 ml	1 tsp	1 tsp
Butter or margarine, cut into pieces	50 g	2 oz	¼ cup
Milk	150 ml	¼ pt	⅔ cup

① Fit the grating disc and grate both cheeses. Remove from the bowl.

② Fit the metal blade. Process the flours, mustard, baking powder and butter or margarine for about 5 seconds until the fat is rubbed in. Add the cheese and process for 3 seconds to combine.

③ With the motor running, pour in the milk through the feed tube until the mixture forms a soft dough.

④ Turn out on to a lightly floured surface, pat into a ball, then roll out to about 1 cm/½ in thick. Cut into rounds with a 5 cm/2 in pastry (cookie) cutter and arrange on a greased baking (cookie) sheet.

⑤ Bake in a preheated oven at 220°C/425°F/gas mark 7 for 10–12 minutes until golden.

PREPARATION AND COOKING TIME: 20 MINUTES

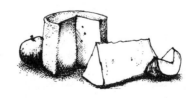

ORANGE FRANGIPANE TARTLETS

—— MAKES ABOUT 24 ——

🌸 4 MONTHS	METRIC	IMPERIAL	AMERICAN
For the pastry (paste):			
Plain (all-purpose) flour	175 g	6 oz	1½ cups
Butter or margarine, cut into pieces	75 g	3 oz	⅓ cup
Grated orange rind	10 ml	2 tsp	2 tsp
Orange juice	30 ml	2 tbsp	2 tbsp
For the filling:			
Butter or margarine, cut into pieces	50 g	2 oz	¼ cup
Caster (superfine) sugar	50 g	2 oz	¼ cup
Egg	1	1	1
Plain flour	25 g	1 oz	¼ cup
Ground almonds	25 g	1 oz	¼ cup
Icing (confectioners') sugar, sifted	100 g	4 oz	½ cup
Water	15 ml	1 tbsp	1 tbsp
Glacé (candied) cherries, halved	12	12	12

① Fit the metal blade. To make the pastry, process the flour, butter or margarine and orange rind for 3–4 seconds until the mixture resembles breadcrumbs. With the motor running, add the orange juice through the feed tube and process for a few seconds until the mixture forms a ball around the blade.

② Turn out on to a lightly floured surface and pull together with the fingertips. Roll out, cut into circles with a 5 cm/2 in pastry (cookie) cutter and use to line 24 greased bun tins (patty pans).

③ To make the filling, process the butter or margarine, sugar, egg, flour and ground almonds for 8–10 seconds until light and fluffy. Spoon the mixture into the pastry cases (pie shells).

④ Bake in a preheated oven at 200°C/400°F/gas mark 6 for 15 minutes until golden. Allow to cool.

⑤ Wash the processor bowl and re-fit the metal blade. Process the icing sugar for a few seconds to break down any lumps. With the motor running, add the water through the feed tube and process for 5–6 seconds until smooth. Spoon the icing (frosting) over the cakes and decorate with cherry halves.

Freezing tip: Freeze without the icing. When required, thaw at room temperature for 2–3 hours, then follow the recipe to finish the icing.

PREPARATION AND COOKING TIME: 20 MINUTES

VIENNESE BISCUITS
—— MAKES ABOUT 12 ——

	METRIC	IMPERIAL	AMERICAN
Almonds	25 g	1 oz	¼ cup
Soft (tub) margarine, cut into pieces	100 g	4 oz	½ cup
Icing (confectioners') sugar, sifted	50 g	2 oz	¼ cup
Plain (all-purpose) flour	100 g	4 oz	1 cup

① Fit the metal blade. Process the almonds for about 20 seconds until finely ground. Add the remaining ingredients and process for 12–14 seconds until the mixture forms a smooth dough.

② Pipe star shapes or place teaspoonfuls of the mixture on to a lightly greased baking (cookie) sheet, allowing space for the mixture to spread.

③ Bake in a preheated oven at 180°C/350°F/gas mark 4 for 10–12 minutes until golden brown around the edges. Allow to cool slightly before removing from the sheet.

PREPARATION AND COOKING TIME: 20 MINUTES

ICED WALNUT BISCUITS

—— MAKES ABOUT 16 ——

✎ ❄ 3 MONTHS	METRIC	IMPERIAL	AMERICAN
Walnuts	75 g	3 oz	¾ cup
Butter or margarine, cut into pieces	100 g	4 oz	½ cup
Soft brown sugar	75 g	3 oz	⅓ cup
Self-raising (self-rising) flour	175 g	6 oz	1½ cups
Icing (confectioners') sugar	50 g	2 oz	¼ cup
Orange juice	15 ml	1 tbsp	1 tbsp

① Fit the metal blade. Process the walnuts for about 6 seconds until finely chopped. Add the butter or margarine, sugar and flour and process for about 20 seconds until the mixture forms a dough around the blade.

② Tip out on to a lightly floured work surface and pull together with the fingertips. Roll out to about 5 mm/¼ in thick, cut out rounds with a fluted 5 cm/2 in biscuit (cookie) cutter and place on a lightly greased baking (cookie) sheet, re-rolling the trimmings until you have used all the dough.

③ Bake in a preheated oven at 180°C/350°F/gas mark 4 for about 15 minutes until evenly browned. Allow to cool a little on the tray before transferring to a cooling rack to finish cooling.

④ Clean the bowl and re-fit the metal blade. Place the icing sugar in the bowl and turn on the motor. Pour the orange juice through the feed tube on to the sugar. Stop and scrape down the sides of the bowl, then process again for 2 seconds to make the icing (frosting). Pipe the icing in lines across the cooled biscuits and leave to set before serving.

PREPARATION AND COOKING TIME: 25 MINUTES

CHOCOLATE CAKE FINGERS

—— MAKES 18–20 ——

🌼 6 MONTHS	METRIC	IMPERIAL	AMERICAN
Eggs	2	2	2
Caster (superfine) sugar	100 g	4 oz	½ cup
Self-raising (self-rising) flour	100 g	4 oz	1 cup
Soft (tub) margarine, cut into pieces	100 g	4 oz	½ cup
Plain (semi-sweet) chocolate	50 g	2 oz	2 oz
Golden (light corn) syrup	15 ml	1 tbsp	1 tbsp
Icing (confectioners') sugar, sifted	50 g	2 oz	¼ cup
Hot water	30 ml	2 tbsp	2 tbsp

① Fit the metal blade. Process the eggs, sugar, flour and margarine for 7–10 seconds until smooth. Turn the mixture into a greased and floured Swiss roll tin (jelly roll pan).

② Bake in a preheated oven at 180°C/350°F/gas mark 4 for 15–20 minutes until golden and springy to the touch. Remove from the tin and leave to cool while you make the icing (frosting).

③ Melt the chocolate in a bowl over a pan of hot water. Put into the processor with the syrup and icing sugar and process for 4–5 seconds until mixed. With the motor running, add the hot water through the feed tube until the mixture is smooth and thick.

④ Spread the warm icing over the cake and mark into a pattern with a fork. Cut the cake into fingers using a bread knife dipped into hot water.

PREPARATION AND COOKING TIME: 35 MINUTES

SHORTBREAD

—— MAKES ABOUT 12 ——

✿ 2 MONTHS	METRIC	IMPERIAL	AMERICAN
Butter, cut into pieces	100 g	4 oz	½ cup
Caster (superfine) sugar	50 g	2 oz	¼ cup
Plain (all-purpose) flour	100 g	4 oz	I cup
Rice flour	25 g	I oz	¼ cup
A little extra caster sugar, for dusting			

① Fit the metal blade. Process the butter and sugar for 15 seconds until well blended. Scrape down the sides, add the flours and process again for 15 seconds until the mixture forms a ball around the blade.

② Turn the dough out on to a lightly floured surface and pull together with your fingertips. Roll out to about 5 mm/¼ in thick and cut into rounds with a 5 cm/2 in biscuit (cookie) cutter.

③ Bake in a preheated oven at 180°C/350°F/gas mark 4 for 15–20 minutes until the biscuits are just golden around the edges. Remove from the oven and sprinkle with caster sugar while still hot.

PREPARATION AND COOKING TIME: 30 MINUTES

CHERRY BISCUITS

—— MAKES ABOUT 12 ——

	METRIC	IMPERIAL	AMERICAN
Plain (all-purpose) flour	175 g	6 oz	1½ cups
Cornflour (cornstarch)	25 g	1 oz	¼ cup
Caster (superfine) sugar	75 g	3 oz	⅓ cup
Soft (tub) margarine, cut into pieces	100 g	4 oz	½ cup
Glacé (candied) cherries	50 g	2 oz	¼ cup
A little extra caster sugar, for sprinkling			

① Fit the metal blade. Process the flour, cornflour and sugar for a few seconds to mix. Add the margarine and process until the mixture looks like fine breadcrumbs. Add the cherries and process very quickly to mix.

② Turn the mixture into a greased and lined Swiss roll tin (jelly roll pan) and press down with your fingertips.

③ Bake in a preheated oven at 160°C/325°F/gas mark 3 for 20–25 minutes until light golden brown. Remove from the oven, sprinkle with caster sugar and mark into fingers. Allow to cool in the tin.

PREPARATION AND COOKING TIME: 35 MINUTES

BASIC RECIPES

Your food processor makes short work of many tasks around the kitchen. It is particularly good for pastry (paste), as you can get the best results quickly and easily. All you have to do is to make sure that you don't overprocess the ingredients

Herb butters are also quick and easy to make. Simply chop your favourite herbs, then process with butter, cut into pieces. Shape into a small dish, or roll into a sausage shape, wrap in greaseproof (waxed) paper, then chill and cut off slices for serving.

A processor is excellent for puréeing baby food. Simply place the food in the processor, moisten with a little milk or stock and process for a few seconds. Rice, pasta, potatoes, meat, chicken, vegetables and fish all process well and as the baby progresses on to lumpier foods, simply process for a shorter time. It is often worthwhile preparing enough food for several baby meals all at once, and then freezing it in tiny quantities in ice-cube trays so that just the right amount can be removed at any one time.

The following basic recipes are included in recipes in the book: breadcrumbs (see page 28); shortcrust pastry (see page 32); choux pastry (see page 100); biscuit (cookie) crumb flan base (see page 101); glacé icing (frosting) (see page 114).

BASIC BREAD
—— MAKES 450 G/1 LB ——

✍	METRIC	IMPERIAL	AMERICAN
Strong plain (bread) flour, warmed	225 g	8 oz	2 cups
Salt	2.5 ml	½ tsp	½ tsp
Butter or margarine	25 g	1 oz	2 tbsp
Sugar	2.5 ml	½ tsp	½ tsp
Fresh yeast	15 g	½ oz	1 tbsp
OR dried yeast	15 ml	1 tbsp	1 tbsp
Milk, warmed	90 ml	6 tbsp	6 tbsp
Water, warmed	45 ml	3 tbsp	3 tbsp

① Fit the metal blade. Place the flour and salt in the processor and add the butter or margarine. Process for 4–5 seconds to rub in the fat.

② If you are using fresh yeast, place it in a jug with the sugar and mix with the back of a spoon until it is a creamy consistency. Gradually stir in the milk and water. If you are using dried yeast, mix it with the sugar, milk and water and leave in a warm place for about 15 minutes until frothy.

③ With the motor running, add the yeast mixture through the feed tube of the food processor and work until a dough is formed. Continue to process for about 40 seconds until the dough is smooth.

④ Turn the dough into an oiled bowl, cover with oiled clingfilm (plastic wrap) and leave in a warm place to rise for about 1 hour until it has doubled in bulk.

⑤ Return the dough to the processor and process for 10–15 seconds to ensure a fine, even texture in the finished bread.

⑥ Shape into a 450 g/1 lb loaf tin (pan), cover and leave to prove for about 1 hour until the dough rises above the top of the tin.

⑦ Bake in a preheated oven at 220°C/425°F/gas mark 7 for about 25 minutes until golden on top and hollow-sounding when tapped on the base.

PREPARATION AND COOKING TIME: 35 MINUTES PLUS RISING

PIZZA DOUGH

—— SERVES 4 ——

🌱 ❄ 3 MONTHS	METRIC	IMPERIAL	AMERICAN
Strong plain (bread) flour	350 g	12 oz	3 cups
Sachet of fast-action dried yeast	1	1	1
A pinch of salt			
A pinch of sugar			
Olive oil	30 ml	2 tbsp	2 tbsp
Warm water	250 ml	8 fl oz	1 cup

① Fit the metal blade and process the flour, yeast, salt and sugar for a few seconds until mixed.

② With the motor running, add the olive oil, then gradually add the warm water until the mixture forms a ball. Process for a further 1 minute to knead the dough.

③ Transfer to an oiled bowl, cover with oiled clingfilm (plastic wrap) and leave in a warm place to rise for about 1 hour.

④ Roll out and use as required.

PREPARATION TIME: 5 MINUTES PLUS RISING

ALMOND PASTE

—— MAKES ENOUGH TO COVER ONE 18 CM/7 IN CAKE ——

🌱	METRIC	IMPERIAL	AMERICAN
Blanched almonds	225 g	8 oz	2 cups
Icing (confectioners') sugar, sifted	175 g	6 oz	¾ cup
Caster (superfine) sugar	175 g	6 oz	¾ cup
Egg	1	1	1
Lemon juice	10 ml	2 tsp	2 tsp
Almond essence (extract)	2 drops	2 drops	2 drops

① Fit the metal blade. Process the almonds for 20–30 seconds until finely ground. Add the sugars, egg, lemon juice and almond essence and process for 10–15 seconds until the mixture forms a smooth ball.

② Wrap in clingfilm (plastic wrap) and chill before using.

PREPARATION TIME: 5 MINUTES

THREE-FRUIT MARMALADE
—— MAKES ABOUT 4 JARS ——

	METRIC	IMPERIAL	AMERICAN
Grapefruit	2	2	2
Oranges	2	2	2
Water	1.2 litres	2 pts	5 cups
Juice of 2 lemons			
Granulated sugar	900 g	2 lb	4 cups

① You need a total of 900 g/2 lb weight of grapefruit and oranges. Place a couple of saucers in the fridge before you start.

② Fit the metal blade. Quarter the grapefruit and remove the skin, pith and pips. Process the grapefruit flesh for 12–15 seconds until finely chopped. Place in a preserving pan.

③ Quarter the oranges, remove the pips and remove the flesh from half the segments. Process this flesh for 10–12 seconds until finely chopped, then add it to the preserving pan.

④ Fit the slicing disc. Slice the remaining orange segments, with the peel on, then add to the preserving pan.

⑤ Collect all the pips, pith and peel in a muslin (cheesecloth) bag, tie securely and place in the preserving pan. Add the water and the juice of the lemons and bring to the boil. Simmer for about 1 hour until the rind is soft.

⑥ Add the sugar and stir over a low heat until dissolved. Bring to the boil and boil rapidly for 5 minutes. Test for setting point by placing 5 ml/1 tsp of the marmalade on a cold saucer and allowing to cool. If the surface wrinkles when gently pressed, the marmalade is ready. If not, boil for another few minutes, then test again.

⑦ Remove from the heat and allow to stand for 10 minutes. Spoon into clean, warm jars, cover and label.

PREPARATION AND COOKING TIME: 2 HOURS

PEANUT BUTTER

—— MAKES 225 g/8 oz ——

🍲	METRIC	IMPERIAL	AMERICAN
Shelled peanuts	225 g	8 oz	2 cups
Oil	10 ml	2 tsp	2 tsp

① Fit the metal place. Process the peanuts for about 20 seconds until they form a paste.

② Scrape down the sides of the bowl, add the oil and process for a further 20 seconds. Store in a screw-topped jar in the fridge.

PREPARATION TIME: 5 MINUTES

RUM BUTTER

—— MAKES 225 g/8 oz ——

🍲	METRIC	IMPERIAL	AMERICAN
Soft brown sugar	100 g	4 oz	½ cup
Butter	100 g	4 oz	½ cup
Rum	10 ml	2 tsp	2 tsp

① Fit the metal blade. Process the sugar and butter for 10–15 seconds until well blended.

② Scrape down the sides of the bowl and add the rum. Process for a further 10–15 seconds until soft and light. Store in small jars in the fridge.

Variation: You can substitute brandy or any other liqueur to make a flavoured butter of your choice. Use caster (superfine) sugar instead of brown for a lighter result if you prefer.

PREPARATION TIME: 5 MINUTES

BUTTER ICING

—— MAKES 225 g/8 oz ——

✎	METRIC	IMPERIAL	AMERICAN
Icing (confectioners') sugar, sifted	175 g	6 oz	¾ cup
Butter, cut into pieces	75 g	3 oz	⅓ cup
A few drops of food colouring or flavouring (optional)			
A little boiling water			

① Fit the metal blade. Place the ingredients in the processor.

② Process for 15–20 seconds until well blended. Stop and scrape down the sides of the bowl with a spatula if necessary.

③ Add the colouring or flavouring, if using, through the feed tube with the motor running and mix until blended.

④ Add a little boiling water, if needed, to make piping easier.

⑤ Turn out the icing (frosting) and use to spread in the centre or over the top of cakes.

Tip: Make sure the butter is at room temperature before you put it in the processor.

PREPARATION TIME: 10 MINUTES

APPLE AND WALNUT STUFFING

—— SERVES 4 ——

	METRIC	IMPERIAL	AMERICAN
Slice of bread	I	I	I
Walnuts	50 g	2 oz	½ cup
Onion, quartered	I	I	I
Eating (dessert) apples, peeled, cored and quartered	2	2	2
Sprigs of parsley	2–3	2–3	2–3
Butter or margarine, cut into pieces	25 g	I oz	2 tbsp
Egg	I	I	I
Salt and freshly ground black pepper			

① Fit the metal blade. With the motor running, drop pieces of bread through the feed to tube to make breadcrumbs. Remove from the bowl.

② Chop the walnuts for 3 seconds until roughly chopped, then remove from the bowl.

③ Process the onion for 2–3 seconds until roughly chopped. Add the apples and process for 4–5 seconds until chopped. Add the breadcrumbs, parsley, butter or margarine, walnuts and egg, and season well with salt and pepper. Process for 2–3 seconds to combine the ingredients.

④ Use as an accompaniment for chicken or pork. Cook in your usual way or roll into small balls and fry (sauté).

PREPARATION TIME: 10 MINUTES

INDEX

0492